PRAGUE
ART AND HISTORY

TIM PORTER

FLOW EAST

© 1991 Flow East Limited, Prague
© text 1991 Tim Porter

Photographs
Jiří Macht, Gordon Hardwick

Design
Carla Sello

Research
Alexandra Miksánkova, Melissa John

Assistance given by
Ministry of Trade and Tourism, National Gallery, National
Museum in Prague, Presidents' Cultural Office - Aura Pont

Produced by Summerfield Press, Florence
Printed in Italy

CONTENTS

In 1464 the Czech King George of Poděbrady sent an important message to the King of France, Louis XI, suggesting that he should form and lead a peaceful league of Christian kings, a defensive association based on the observation of international rights to prevent warfare between the member states and to guarantee their defence. In my opinion it was not by accident that one of the first serious attempts to create a peaceful Europe should have originated in Central Europe. Historically this region has always been the focus of European conflicts and it is therefore understandable that it should show a strong interest in peace and security for Europe as a whole.

In our country we have freedom of opinion and belief: for the first time since World War II all Catholic dioceses are headed by a bishop and the monastic orders are active again. Our state has no state ideology. The only idea that inspires our internal and international policies is an idea based on the respect of human rights in general and of the uniqueness of each individual human being.

We feel that we are a sovereign state and we want to live in friendship with all nations all over the world.

VÁCLAV HAVEL
President of the CSFR

From a speech delivered before the European Parliament at Strasbourg, 10 May 1990. This extract is quoted with the permission of the President's Office in Prague.

INTRODUCTION

Prague is a city of the unexpected. Rich in mythology, one only has to stand in the middle of Charles Bridge at dead of night amongst the moon shadows cast by the early Gothic bridge towers and Baroque statues to appreciate something of the special atmosphere of the place. Despite her turbulent history, which has seen her placed on more than one occasion at the burning edge of ideological frictions, Prague has emerged with the main fabric of her architectural wealth intact. From Malá Strana, with its cobbled squares lined with the Baroque palaces of the illustrious elite, through the tortuous meanderings of the alleys flowing amongst the Gothic market squares of Staroměstske, to the looming shadows of Hradčany Castle that raises St. Vitus skyward like a chalice held aloft to the heavens, there is always something of interest close at hand. As the swans glide past on the wide waters of the Vltava, over the rippling reflections of turrets and domes, or skeins of mist drape themselves between her seven hills to be punctured by spires and steeples, Prague challenges us to know the unknowable.

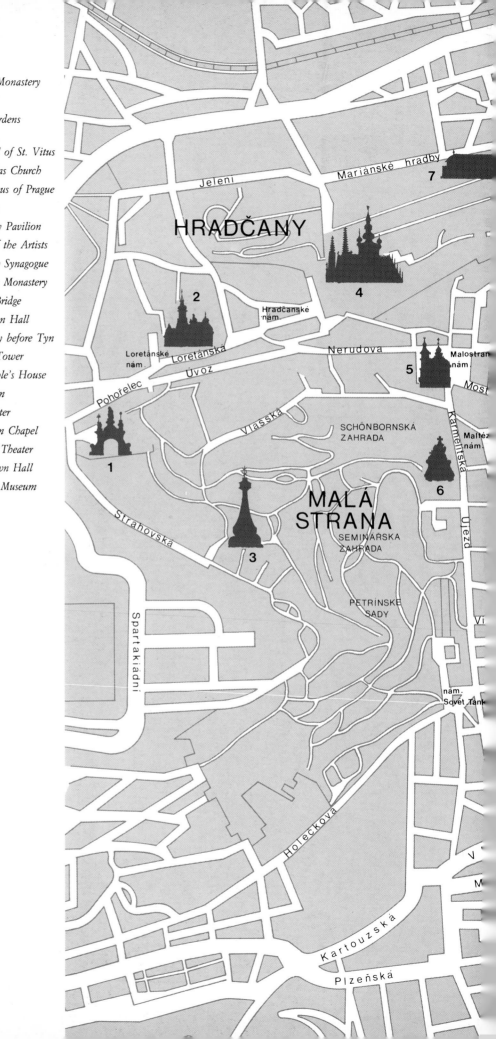

1. Strahovský klášter — *Strahov Monastery*
2. Loreta — *Loreto*
3. Růžovy sad — *Rose Gardens*
4. Pražsky hrad + Katedrala Sv. Vita — *Castle + Cathedral of St. Vitus*
5. Sv. Mikuláše — *St. Nicolas Church*
6. Pražské Jezulátko — *Infant Jesus of Prague*
7. Belveder — *Belvedere*
8. Hanavský pavilón — *Hanavsky Pavilion*
9. Dům umělců — *House of the Artists*
10. Staronová synagoga — *Old New Synagogue*
11. Anežský klášter — *St. Agnes Monastery*
12. Karlův most — *Charles Bridge*
13. Staroměstská radnice — *Old Town Hall*
14. Týnský chrám — *Our Lady before Tyn*
15. Prašná brána — *Powder Tower*
16. Lidóvý dům — *The People's House*
17. Karolinum — *Carolinum*
18. Tylovo divadlo — *Tyl Theater*
19. Betlémská kaple — *Bethlehem Chapel*
20. Národní divadlo — *National Theater*
21. Novoměstaká radnice — *New Town Hall*
22. Narodní muzeun — *National Museum*

Charles Bridge at night.

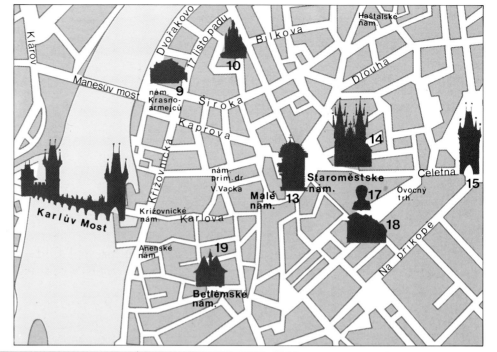

STARÉ MĚSTO · THE OLD TOWN

The area now known as the Old Town was the centre of
Romanesque Prague. Here, where the road joining Prague Castle with
Vyšehrad intersected the ancient east-west trade route, there grew up
an important commercial centre, on a site close to the present Old
Town Square. The merchants who settled here in the twelfth century
stood to profit not only from international trade but also from the
commerce in luxury goods to service the requirements of the royal
courts. At this early stage the settlement was not yet a town in the
medieval sense of the word as it possessed no town charter and,
perhaps more importantly for the security of the inhabitants, no
town walls.

With the accession of Wenceslas I in 1230 a charter recognizing the
rights of the inhabitants was finally granted and the area now borded
by the streets Národní, Na Příkopě and Revoluční was surrounded by
a double wall and a moat. The name of the street Na Příkopě
(literally "on the moat") is a modern reminder of these ancient
fortifications. Preserved in the foyer of the Můstek underground
station are the remains of the original stone bridge that spanned the
moat. This stretch of walls was further fortified by thirteen towers
and gateways, none of which unfortunately have survived, although
their location is recalled by the thirteen streets which enter the Old
Town from the main thoroughfares mentioned above.

The **Powder Tower** (Prašná Brána) still stands on the western side of
Náměstí Republiky at the entrance to the medieval street Celetná.
Originally a late Gothic tower, dating from the end of the fifteenth
century, it stands on the site of one of the earlier gateways in honour
of the newly elected King Vladislav Jagiello (1471-1516), a member
of the Polish royal family. Financed by the inhabitants of the Old
Town, work started in 1475 though four hundred years were to
elapse before its completion. In 1484 the builders laid down their
tools when Vladislav transferred his residence from the neighbouring
Royal Court to Prague Castle, a move prompted by increasingly
volatile relations between the townspeople and the patriciate who
were attempting to reintroduce Catholicism. The uncompleted tower
was furnished with a temporary roof and served as a store for
gunpowder until the end of the seventeenth century giving us the
name by which it is known today. It is easy to be fooled by the
purist Neo-Gothic reconstructions carried out in Prague by Josef
Mocker in the late nineteenth century and the Powder Tower is no
exception. Although the ornamental decoration of Matěj Rejsek,
Prague's principal late Gothic architect alongside Benedikt Ried, is

Page 6
The Old Town from the
roof of the National
Theatre.

Page 8
The Gothic taste for
sculptural ornament is very
much in evidence on the
Powder Tower.

still very much in evidence, much of the present character of the tower, including the hip roof, is the result of Mocker's work, necessitated largely by the damage incurred during the Prussian siege of the city in 1737.

Adjoining the tower to the right is the unmistakable Secessionist splendour of the **People's House** (Obecní Dům). Until 1679 the site was occupied by the buildings of the Royal Court (although they ceased to function as such in 1484). These were severely damaged by the fire that ravaged the Old Town in the same year; after it was rebuilt the complex housed an archiepiscopal seminary and later a barracks and school for cadets. The present building was erected between 1906 and 1912 at a time when Czech artists and architects were held in the thrall of the anti-historical style of Art Nouveau, which took its decorative motifs not from the well-thumbed vocabulary of historical antecedents, but from the mother of all invention, Nature herself.

Enter the Old Town via Celetná, one of the oldest streets in Prague and you join what is undoubtedly the main promenade of the city. Suddenly everyone seems to be going in the same direction, following not only the ancient east-west trade route but also that of the coronation procession, which cut a swathe through the mostly circuitous medieval streets on its way from the Royal Court to St. Vitus Cathedral. Every inch of the journey is steeped in history, some of its moments more glorious than others. Prague still has many well-kept secrets. The cores of Gothic and Renaissance buildings lie hidden behind the doors of some of the houses, their earlier ancestry belied by subsequent Baroque and Neo-Classical accretions. Two such buildings are the high Baroque palaces of **Hrzán** and **Buquoy**. If you look hard enough though, some benign power has afforded us glimpses into the more distant past. In the gateway of number 17, **Menhart House**, for example, we can still see a small bricked-up portal from the fourteenth century. Look high up on the facade of number 13, **Caretto Millesimo Palace**, and you will see two brick-built Gothic side gables.

But for those gasps of wonder that only an unexpected confrontation with the ancient past can procure we have to venture underground. Towards the end of the thirteenth century the frequent flooding of the Vltava had proved such a nuisance that it was decided to raise the ground level of the whole Old Town by two to three metres. This, together with the building boom generated by the new urban rights at the time of Wenceslas I and a devastating fire in 1291, meant that Gothic Prague grew up literally on top of its Romanesque predecessor, swallowing the ground floors of the old stone houses whole and consigning them to a clandestine life beneath the new street level. These two facts, the preponderance of stone built architecture and the artificial raising of the ground level, reflect the ever increasing prosperity of the Old Town. Many of these basements have only relatively recently been discovered and now serve as restaurants and clubs, such as **U zlatého jelena** (The Golden Stag) or **U Sixtu** (At the House of Sixth, No. 2), both in Celetná. The most important of these subterranean time capsules, however, is the originally Romanesque **Palace of George of Poděbrady** in

The Secessionist splendour of the People's House.

The Old Town Square.

Řetězová. Without doubt the largest of the Romanesque structures preserved in the cellarage of the Old Town, the palace, with its vaulting springing from central piers, provides a clear idea of the layout and construction techniques employed in the domestic stone architecture of the day.

The effect of leaving Celetná and entering the majestic space of the **Old Town Square** is somewhat akin to what a log must feel having ridden white waters to be jettisoned from an estuary mouth into the still expanse of the ocean. Yet its beauty and noble proportions belie some of the grim moments from the city's history. In 1422 the square provided the backdrop for the execution of Jan Želivský, a Hussite radical responsible for inciting his fellows during the first Prague defenestration in 1419, thereby provoking the Hussite wars. Sixteen years later it was the scene for Hussite reprisals on a wider scale when Jan Roháč of Dubé was put to death along with 56 of his comrades. In 1621 the twenty-seven leaders of the Protestant anti-Habsburg uprising were executed as a final and dramatic warning that all attempts to resist the monarchical autocracy and the reintroduction of Catholicism were doomed to failure.

All the major streets that enter the Old Town are drawn inexorably

towards this the ancient commercial epicentre like the individual silken threads of a mighty web. The first markets in the area were actually held in the **Týn Ungelt**, a walled trading centre dating from 1135 and situated between the churches of Our Lady before Týn and St. James. At this time the largest market contained within the Old Town walls was in the Gall Town. This initially autonomous settlement was founded in 1232 and granted a royal charter around 1234 as part of Wenceslas I's progressive programme of urbanization. The rights and privileges of the two towns were unified in 1287; at about the same time the craftsmen were organizing themselves into a brotherhood which in due course became a guild. The growth of trade at the end of the thirteenth century led to the setting up of specialized market places and to the codification of the rights and duties of foreign merchants at a time when life in the Old Town was centred around four main squares; Staroměstske (Old Town), Havelské (Gall Town), Kozí (The Goat) and Mariánské (The Virgin Mary). There was still no real form of self administration, however, the reins being held by the Royal Magistrate directly appointed by and responsible to the King. In 1296 the Prague patriciate, who had grown wealthy from trading in silver extracted from the mines at

The Old Town Hall Tower affords a superb view across the Old Town.

17

St. James Church: Baroque ornamental sculpture above the left door.

Kutná Hora, petitioned Wenceslas II for permission to build a town hall and appoint a town clerk. The King, eager to maintain a direct hold on the affairs of the Old Town, approved only the appointment of the clerk. The boot was on the other foot, however, when Wenceslas, keen to raise the international status of Prague, sought support from the baronial Estates to found a university. The barons, realizing that it was legal studies in France and Italy which provided ambitious monarchs with the necessary arguments and expertise to construct a more centralized rule, successfully frustrated his plans. The townspeople had to wait until 1338 for the right to build their own town hall. This was finally granted by John of Luxemburg in return for their financing of his adventurous foreign exploits. This town hall, which is really an agglomeration of buildings purchased and adapted over a period of time, is now the focus of the Old Town Square, not least because of the renowned **Astronomical Clock** set in the western facade of the tower. The clock in its earliest form dates from about 1410 and is attributed to Mikuláš of Kadaň. A morbid legend relates how Wenceslas IV (1378-1419) had him blinded so that the remarkable feat of engineering should never be repeated. Although it is not true, the mere fact that such a story

*The renowned
Astronomical Clock.*

*The characteristic, multi-
turreted towers of the
Church of Our Lady before
Týn echo those of the Old
Town Hall.*

Old Town Hall - the Renaissance window.

Ornamental door in the Old Town.

should be invented is a reflection of the low esteem in which Wenceslas IV was held by the populace, but then he did have the misfortune of acceding to the position held by his glorious father, the Holy Roman Emperor Charles IV. He was not, by the way, the Good King Wenceslas of British Christmas tradition: it was St. Wenceslas, made Duke of Bohemia in 921, who had earned himself this term of endearment. The function of the clock was perfected in 1490 by Hanuš of Růže and displays just about everything regarding time and its relationship with the Heavens that you should ever need to know.

The upper face is split into four main zones, the blue referring to day, the black to night and the two brown areas to dawn and dusk. The outer ring bears the twenty-four hour clock of normal Czech usage, the inner the anti-meridian and post-meridian in Roman numerals. The smaller inset face displays the signs of the zodiac and the respective positions of the Sun, Moon and Pole Star. The lower calendar face, a copy of the one executed by Josef Manes in 1866 (the original now resides in the entrance hall of the Municipal Museum), is decorated with beautiful allegorical paintings of the months of the year. Around its edge are displayed the names of all the Saints for every day of the year. On the hour, every hour until ten in the evening, the crowds gather like disciples round a prophet to witness the ritualistic dance of the figures next to the main clock

"Praga - Caput - Regni."

Renaissance sgraffito decoration on the House at the Minute.

Clam Gallas Palace.

Štorch's House.

face and receive solemn benediction from the twelve apostles as they file past the two door openings at the top. As the figure of Death tolls his knell, the Turk on his left shakes his head denying that his time is up. The Turk was a popular subject of loathing at a time when the Ottoman Empire had expanded to include the lowlands of Hungary, thereby constituting a very real threat to the Czech domains. On the other side meanwhile, the miser feebly shakes his stick and bag of gold as the vain man admires his reflection in the looking glass.

Most of the interior of the Old Town Hall is only accessible by joining one of the guided tours that depart from the foyer on the

The richly decorated façade of Rott's House.

hour, after the striking of the clock. Situated next to the clock tower is the main entrance portal, where once more we can discern the hand of Matěj Rejsek in the intricate carving of figures and flora on the frame. The ornamental decoration of doorways became a prominent feature of Prague architectural embellishment, and so many of the entrances to palaces are guarded by monumental figural sculpture that it is a wonder the night air is not filled with their stone groans. Further along to the left is the beautiful **House at the Minute**, one of the most recent buildings acquired for use as part of the Town Hall in 1886. Originally a Gothic structure, it was rebuilt during the Renaissance when it received its sgraffito decoration,

Nineteenth-century painted decoration in Myslikova.

Right
The majestic spires of the Church of Our Lady before Týn rise up behind the Týn School and the House at the White Unicorn.

portraying classical and biblical scenes as well as allegorical figures of the Virtues. The pictorial decoration of building facades is another characteristic feature of Prague which, although frowned on by the intellectualizing of the Baroque, came back into vogue with Art Nouveau at the end of the nineteenth and beginning of the twentieth centuries. There are two fine examples in the vicinity of the Old Town Square; one at **Štorch's House** (No.16) and the other in the Malé Náměstí at **Rott's House** (No.3). In the fifteenth century a printing press was located here which produced the first Bible in the Czech language in 1488.

The top of the clock tower affords a remarkable view of the whole of the Old Town. From here the meandering network of medieval streets reveals how the district took shape not as the result of some grandiose, far-sighted planning but rather in response to the needs of the day. **The Church of Our Lady before Týn** (Kostel P. Marie před Týnem) looms mightily from behind the Gothic buildings which close the square to the east. **The Týn School** and adjacent **House at the White Unicorn** (Dům U bílého jednorožce) almost seem to cower in her presence as they deny her access to the square below. It may seem odd that the largest and most beautiful church in the Old Town should not open directly onto the square that it so obviously dominates with her many turreted steeples, so distinctive a feature of the Prague skyline. This is due to the fact that the original church on this site, a much smaller structure dating from 1135, was built by the hospice of foreign merchants in the Týn Ungeld and was never intended to be a feature of the Old Town Square. By the late

Peter Parler's tympanum from the Church of Our Lady before Týn. National Gallery, Convent of St. George.

Right
Golz-Kinský Palace.

The Church of Our Lady before Týn seen through the arcade at the top of the Old Town Hall Tower.

fourteenth century, when it started to be rebuilt in its present form on the previously consecrated site, the early Gothic cores of the buildings which front it today were already in place.

Construction work on the church started in 1365, during the reign of Charles IV. By the 1380s the choir along with the arches and walls of the main and lateral naves were completed. The north portal with its exquisitely carved tympanum depicting scenes from Christ's Passion (original now in the National Gallery's collection of Bohemian art situated next to the Basilica of St. George in Prague Castle) is the work of Peter Parler, Prague's foremost Gothic architect. During the Hussite wars (1419-34) this was the main town church where, from 1424, Jan Rokycana, later to become the first Hussite Archbishop, delivered his sermons to the attentive congregation. Under the elected Hussite King George of Poděbrady the church was finally finished with the construction of the west gable and the addition of the two steeples. Originally this was surmounted by a statue of the king with a drawn sword and a golden chalice, a symbol of the Utraquist doctrine. These, together with the words "The Truth Prevails," were summarily removed after the Battle of the White Mountain in 1620 — a grimly ironic portent for the prevailing conditions of more recent years.

Entrance to the church is gained through the Týn School in front of the west facade. Like so many other churches in Prague the original

Gothic appearance of the interior has succumbed to the overwhelming influence of the Baroque. Damage caused by the Great Fire of 1679 meant that the main vault had to be replaced although, thankfully, the Gothic vaulting of the lateral naves has been preserved intact. Behind a Gothic pulpit dating from the fifteenth century stands the marble tombstone of the celebrated Danish astronomer Tycho de Brahe. Brahe came to Prague in 1597, where he took up the position of Court Astronomer to Emperor Rudolf II in 1599. The observations he made while here in Prague were used by Johannes Kepler, another astronomer brought to the city at Rudolf's behest, as the basis for his laws on the movement of the planets. Kepler's laws, however, which related to the movement of the planets round the sun, were in contrast with geocentric view of the universe held by Brahe. The high altar bears a panel depicting the Ascension of our Lady and the Holiest Trinity by Karel Škréta (1649), the leading exponent of Baroque painting whose works decorate a large number of original and restyled Baroque churches. Nestling in between the Týn School and the Golz-Kinský Palace with its exuberant Rococo facade the **House at the Stone Bell** strikes a note of cool, Gothic dignity. During the reign of John of Luxemburg (1310-1348) the early Gothic building was transformed into this monumental tower and probably functioned as a town palace for Queen Elizabeth, daughter of Wenceslas II. The richly decorated

27

The Gothic House at the Stone Bell adds to the architectural diversity of the Old Town Square.

window linings and statuary niches on the exterior had been preserved for centuries beneath a Baroque facade which, following extensive architectural and archaeological research from 1973-87, was removed and the building restored to its former Gothic glory. The interior, with preserved fragments of delicate early Gothic frescoes, now houses temporary exhibitions from the National Gallery's collection of graphic art.

Returning to the square one should mention that its proportions look slightly different today to how they did before the 8th May 1945 when, during the Prague uprising, the Nazis razed the Neo-Gothic east wing of the Town Hall to the ground. Under the Communists

The Baroque Church of St. Nicholas dominates the northern corner of the Old Town Square.

there were supposed to have been plans to reconstruct the area now marked by a long patch of grass but to this day nothing has been done. This is perhaps no bad thing for the harmonious eclecticism of the square is enhanced by the presence of the finely proportioned Baroque facade of the **Church of St. Nicholas** (1732-35), which was previously consigned to relative ignominy in the narrow street of U Radnice. The architect of this church was Killian Ignaz Dietzenhofer, who went on to create the masterly Church of St. Nicholas in the Malá Strana.

On the north side of the square the sombre sculptural grouping of the **Jan Hus Monument** has surveyed the scene since it was set in

Looking up into the dome of St. Nicholas in the Old Town.

place in 1915 to commemorate the 500th anniversary of the martyrdom of the leader of the Hussite reform movement. In 1968 when the tanks of the Warsaw Pact rolled into the square to put an end to the liberalist tendencies that occasioned the Prague Spring, the monument was draped in black, mourning the loss of new-found liberties.

Any of the riddle of medieval streets that run south from the coronation route, as it continues into the Malé Náměstí down Jilská and right into Karlova, are worth exploring. Jilská, Michalská and Melantrichova are all interconnected by Gothic and Renaissance alleyways which run through the typically deep medieval building plots. In fact, if you have time to spare, it is almost worth throwing your map away and pitting your wits and nose for direction against

50 YEARS OF THE
BIG-BLOCK CHEVY

HOT ROD

20 LS INTAKE MANIFOLDS **DYNO TESTED!**

THE MYSTERY EXPOSED

HOW MICKEY
THOMPSON, ZORA
ARKUS-DUNTOV,
AND SMOKEY
YUNICK REALLY
RACED
THE FIRST
427ci
MYSTERY
MOTORS
IN 1963
CORVETTES—
AND CHEVY
NEVER
WANTED YOU
TO KNOW!
AND ONLY HOT ROD
COULD REUNITE
M/T'S CAR WITH
YUNICK'S ENGINE
AND TAKE THEM
BACK OUT ON
THE TRACK FOR
THE FIRST TIME
IN 52-YEARS!

INSIDE:
WORLD'S
QUICKEST
AND FASTEST
SMALL-
BLOCK
CHEVYS

HOT ROD WHERE IT ALL BEGAN

CRATE ENGINE **EVOLUTION**

FIRST LAPS **VIPER ACR**

42ci PONTIAC **GIANT KILLER**

AEROSPACE-SPEC **RAT MOTOR**

DECEMBER 2015

**TOP
SPEED
TESTED!**
FORDS,
PONTIACS
& CHEVYS
ALL TRY TO RUN
MORE THAN
221 MPH PG. 46

THE ENTHUSIAST NETWORK

TEN

EVERY DAY

IF YOU NEEDED A PICTURE, YOU WEREN'T GOING TO BUY ONE ANYWAY

the narrow and winding streets which almost constitute a living maze. Just past No. 18 Jilská, a passageway opens up on the left which leads through a palace courtyard with Renaissance arcades and into the end of Michalská. Bear left and the alley opens into another courtyard, this time containing the dilapidated Baroque **Church of St. Michael**. The former Gothic church which stood on this site was home at various times throughout the fifteenth century to a succession of Hussite preachers, including Jan Hus himself. The Servite monastery (1636-64), of which the church was a part, was abolished like so many others under Emperor Josef II, in an ambitious attempt to subjugate the Catholic Church to his rule. Once you emerge into Melantrichova, take a right and follow the street a short distance till it is crossed by Havelská. The area

Ladislav Saloun's monument to Jan Hus, set up in 1915 to commemorate the 500th anniversary of his martyrdom.

enclosed by this street and those that run parallel to it between the Uhelný trh (Coal Market) to the west and the Ovocný trh (Fruit Market) to the east, housed the immense Gall market, known as the New Market at its foundation to distinguish it from the one already in existence on the Old Town Square. Standing at the Uhelný trh end and looking up towards the **Church of St. Gall (Kostel svatého Havla)** the original proportions of the square can still be discerned despite the intrusion of subsequent building developments, which, although they bisected it, thankfully preserved the long runs of Gothic arcading. Here, medieval merchants laid out their wares protected from the intrusive inclemency of the weather. The Gothic church which stood on the site of the present Baroque structure of St. Gall was at the time one of the most important churches in the whole of Prague and acted as the parish church for the Gall Town. From 1363 to 1369 it was the scene for the reformist, puritanical sermons preached by Konrad Waldhauser, who had been invited to Prague with the approval of Charles IV by the first Archbishop, Ernest of Pardubice.

Behind the church, at the junction of Rytířská and Železná, stands the Neo-Classical **Tyl Theatre** which was opened in 1783 as the Nostitz Theatre. It was here on 29th October 1787 that the world premiere of Mozart's *Don Giovanni* took place, written especially for his Prague audience who, in contrast to the Viennese, had received *The Marriage of Figaro* with rapturous enthusiasm. While in Prague, Mozart stayed with the Dušek family in their villa **Bertramka**, situated in Mozartova in the Smíchov district of the city; the building now houses the Mozart Museum.

Next to the Tyl Theatre, at Železná No.9, stands the **Carolinum**, the core of the university founded by Charles IV in 1348, and the first in Central Europe. Although the hub of its activities is now located here, at its foundation there was no permanent site, lectures taking place in churches and monasteries and even in the houses of the masters themselves. It was not until 1383 that the university found a permanent home with the donation by Wenceslas IV of the Gothic house of the Master of the Mint, Jan Rotlev. Like the Town Hall, the original Gothic buildings of the Carolinum developed organically, additions to the complex being made by the purchase of surrounding buildings, which were then adapted to serve their new function. The beautiful Gothic oriel window which protrudes from the Baroque southern facade is by the workshop of Peter Parler, also responsible for the oriel of the chapel in the Old Town Hall.

The university was split into four administrative bodies catering for the scholars of different nationalities who came to study here — the Czechs, the Poles, the Saxons and the Bavarians — and, in the universal spirit of the times, the four groups were also symbolic of the four points of the compass. In 1398 Jan Hus was appointed to the university as Professor of Philosophy. From this time on it became the forum for hotly contested debates regarding the divisions between secular and religious power and the widespread, virulent corruption within the Catholic Church.

In the delicate balance between secular and religious authority, ecclesiastical offices were more often than not awarded in the spirit

The spires of St. Gall.

St. Martin's is the oldest preserved rotunda in Prague.

of political expediency. It was a time of crisis within the Roman Catholic Church. The Holy See was transferred to Avignon to escape the bloody internal feuds rife in Rome at the time, giving rise to the great schism of dual papacy which was to last until 1415.

The seeds of reform had taken root following the closer contact with England, engendered by the marriage of Anna, a daughter of Charles IV, to King Richard II in 1381. Czech students, returning from study periods at Oxford University, brought with them the books of John Wyclif which provided the philosophical basis for a return to a religious piety in concordance with the original teachings of the Bible. These ideas were not well received by the other nations who were in a majority at the university nor, not surprisingly, by the clergy. The church, already weakened by the schism of dual papacy, was not keen to have its power undermined still further by the advance of popular reform. In any case, Hus was safe for the time being from reprisals by the Church, enjoying as he did the patronage of Wenceslas IV. The Archbishop of Prague supported the Roman Pope in opposition to Wenceslas, who favoured the Pope-elect in Pisa. The Archbishop, who needed the King's support to bring action against Hus, was powerless while they continued to conflict over this point. Hus reinforced his position when he managed to persuade the King to alter the voting structure within the university, thanks to the decree of Kutná Hora in 1409 which gave the Bohemians three votes to the other nations' one. Four years later, however, Hus's position became extremely precarious, because he frustrated the King's plans by condemning the sacrilegious sale of indulgences, the proceeds of which were intended to help finance the war of the Pisan Pope against the Pope in Rome. Fearing possible repercussions, Hus left Prague and spent two years in the protection of his friends from the minor nobility. In his absence the reform party became more radical under the direction of Jakoubek of Stříbro, who declared the Pope an Antichrist and instigated the serving of the the Holy Communion in both ways (*sub utraque specie* — which led to the reformers also being known as Utraquists).

Until then the lay people could only partake of the body of Christ at Communion, the blood being reserved expressly for the clergy, as their privilege.

Hus came out of hiding in 1415 to defend his views at the Council of Constance, having accepted a guarantee of safe conduct from Emperor Sigismund. This, however, proved to be worthless. In Constance he was arrested and sentenced to be burnt at the stake for holding the Wyclifite heresies. After his martyrdom Hus was venerated as a saint, and the reform movement, which previously had been known as Wyclifite, took on the name Hussite, although the reformers were also called Utraquist or Calixtines after their symbol, a chalice.

The church where the first Utraquist communion took place, St. Martin in the Wall, is tucked away in Martinská, a street which runs out of Uhelný trh to the west. The original Romanesque church on this site, dating from 1178, the nave of which is preserved in the present church, served the needs of a village community that spread southwards in the direction of the present New Town.

Rotunda of the Holy Cross.

At that time the little Romanesque churches were not part of a unified town complex but rather stood as the focus of small individual village communities, the real process of urbanization being restricted to the area around the Old Town Square. Apart from the Romanesque elements preserved in the basements of later Gothic houses, architectural reminders of that prosperous period in the Old Town are extremely scant. Around this time there were for example twenty Romanesque rotundas of which only three have survived: one in the New Town, **St. Longinus** in Na Rybníčku; one at Vyšehrad, **St. Martin's**; and one here in the Old Town, the **Rotunda of the Holy Cross** (sv.Kříž) in Karoliny Světlé.

When the Romanesque settlements were surrounded by walls in 1231, the builders where possible made use of the natural defensive opportunities afforded by the terrain. Consequently, the **Church of St. Martin in the Wall** was separated from the village and even included in the fortifications, resulting in the rather bizarre name by which it has been known to the present day. The appearance of the church today is a result of the late Gothic reconstruction carried out before 1488, when two lateral naves were added to the building which had already been enlarged by the addition of a square presbytery in about 1350. Set into the wall of this is a commemorative plaque to the famous Brokoff family of sculptors, who left their mark not only on the avenue of statues on Charles Bridge but also on the figural decoration of palace facades — a representative feature of Prague Baroque.

Carrying on past the church, Martinská leads into Na Perštýně which was part of the old route connecting the two castles of Vyšehrad and Hradčany. Take a right and you are heading back towards the coronation route. About 100 yards to the left, Bethlehem Square opens off Husova. You can't miss the twin gabled roof of the Bethlehem Chapel, with its austere facade, a blunt rejection of the intricate sculptural ornamentation favoured in secular and established church projects, recalling the fact that this was the centre of the reform movement, the embryonic Hussites. Although this is a modern reconstruction from 1954, the original church of 1381 having run to ruin, it is faithful to the plans of its historic predecessor. You might ask why the Communist government of the day should spend money on such a restoration project when they followed a largely atheistic policy which resulted in the defrocking of many priests, consigning them to menial labour, and the expulsion of others. The majority of smaller churches were closed and they now wait sadly for renovation, like derelict amnesiacs hoping that their memories might one day be restored to them. In fact the rebuilding of the chapel was sanctioned by the first Communist President and Prime Minister, Klement Gottwald, on the grounds that in 1521 the German peasant figurehead, Thomas Münzer, had preached here, illustrating his prophetic vision of a communistic state: Gottwald felt that this made it ideal as a monument to the long history of Communist ideals in Prague.

Continuing up Husova, we come to one of the few churches in the Old Town to have preserved its original Gothic exterior. The construction of the **Church of St. Giles** (sv. Jilji) was begun by the

Bishop of Prague, Jan of Dražice, around 1310 and completed by the Archbishop, Ernest of Pardubice, in 1371. Jan of Dražice was an enthusiastic propagator of the new Gothic style with which he had become acquainted during his long stay at the Papal Court in Avignon. In Prague the Gothic had not been filtered through Germany but derived directly from France where it had originated; the earliest Gothic buildings in the city were built by Cistercian masons from Burgundy. As more and more people moved into the town they were followed by various monastic orders, many of whom, in the ongoing atmosphere of moral disintegration, lived in a profligate manner, falling victim to the vices that accompanied the more variegated urban lifestyle.

The Convent of St. Agnes (a visit to which is best combined with a tour of Josefov) is a case in point: here nuns and monks lived in such close proximity that it was only a matter of time before suspicions were aroused. The convent was founded in 1233 by Wenceslas I at the instigation of his sister Agnes of Bohemia. Agnes introduced the Order of the Poor Clares, the female branch of the Franciscan order, into Bohemia and in 1235 she became abbess of the newly constructed convent. The nuns originally had the use of the adjacent **Church of St. Francis**, but around 1240 monks from the recently completed Minorite monastery took over the church whose windows apparently looked through into the dormitory of the nuns! Thus denied their place of worship, the nuns set about building a new church which was later enlarged by the addition of a presbytery and consecrated to the Holy Saviour in the 1280s. Agnes herself was buried here along with other members of the Premsylid dynasty whose crowned heads form the sculptural decoration on the large capitals of the columns supporting the triumphal arch of the church. Various alterations were carried out during the fourteenth century, including the addition of an extra storey to the wings of the cloister and the construction of a steeple and chapel dedicated to St. Barbara in the Church of St. Francis. This chapel was badly damaged in the fire of 1689 after which it was given the Baroque restoration which has survived to the present day.

During the Protestant Hussite uprising of 1420 the Catholic sisters fled for their lives, leaving the convent deserted for well over a century. From 1556 to 1626 it was occupied by the Dominicans, who had been ejected by the Jesuits from the monastery at St. Clement. The Poor Clares finally returned in 1627 when their fears had possibly been allayed by the Imperial ordinance of that year which made Catholicism the only permissible religion. In 1782 the convent was finally abolished and converted into a storehouse and dwelling place for the poor. Today many of the convent buildings have been restored to their former Gothic glory and house part of the collection of the National Gallery.

The number of monastic orders, invited from abroad, increased during the reign of Charles IV, a policy designed to enhance the prestige and reflect the international religious importance of the city, now that it had become the capital of the Holy Roman Empire. These supplemented the Franciscans and Dominicans who had already established themselves within the precincts of the Old Town

Left
The Church of St. Giles rises up above the bluff of the Old Town.

Carved pews in St. Giles.

39

— the Franciscans between the Convent of the Blessed Agnes (Agnes was only canonized in 1990) and the **Church of St. James** (sv. Jakub), and the Dominicans around the **Church of St. Clement** (sv. Kliment) in Karlova. Incidentally, the acoustics in St. James are so remarkable that the organ in this church simply *has* to be heard.

The Dominicans were displaced when the Jesuits were summoned to Prague by the Habsburgs, in their remorseless battle to reinstitute Catholicism. Between 1556 and 1593 they systematically purchased land and property around the Church of St. Clement over an area of two hectares to make way not only for the Church of the Holy Saviour on Crusader Knights Square, but also for the massive expanse of the Jesuit College of the **Clementinum**.

In the area now encompassed by its walls there once stood about twenty-five houses as well as several churches and the monastery buildings attached to the original church of St. Clement, after which the complex was named. The expansionist doctrine of the Jesuits eventually led to their taking over of the Carolinum in 1656, when it was merged with the Clementinum to become the Charles-Ferdinand University. Although the exterior, articulated only by a rather monotonous ranging of Corinthian pilasters, is somewhat subdued (with the exception of the southern facade which is enlivened by the presence of the rotunda of the Italian Chapel between the Holy Saviour and St. Clement), in the interior three rooms in particular retain the magnificence of the high Baroque. The first, known as the **Baroque Hall**, houses the State Library of Czechoslovakia and is decorated with ceiling frescoes of the Muses and impressive *trompe l'oeil* compositions by J.Hiebl (1727), while the second, the **Mathematical Hall**, adorned with original Rococo stucco work, holds a permanent exhibition of eighteenth-century table clocks. Beneath the dome of the **Astronomical Tower** are displayed some of the mathematical and astronomical instruments used in the experiments of Tycho de Brahe.

There are times in Prague when, despite the grandeur of the Baroque, one cannot but help being reminded of the wholesale destruction that took place to accommodate the redevelopment. But there are also times when the Baroque, applied sensitively, achieved a rare harmony with earlier existing structures. One example of this is the recently restored **House at The Golden Well** (Dům U zlaté studně) on the corner of Seminářská and Karlova, where the application of Baroque stucco reliefs of popular saints enhances the simple lines of the Renaissance structure.

You will have noticed by now that the majority of houses are referred to by their romantic, folklorish signs. As in so many fields, the romantic sufferred at the hands of the rational, when in the mid-eighteenth century Empress Maria Theresa urged the allocation of house numbers to replace the beautiful but outmoded mediaeval system. But although the postal system is governed numerically, numbers and pictures co-exist peacefully on the exteriors of many buildings. Golden is an epithet that abounds — At the Golden Tree (U zlatého stromu), At the Golden Tiger (U zlatého tygra), At the Golden Scales (U zlaté váhy) — its use originating in Rudolfinian literature, where Caroline Prague became the "Golden City." This referred in particular to the gilding of the roofs of the castle gates carried out by Charles IV so that they might act as beacons, visible from great distances, declaring the fame and prosperity of the city. Thereafter its popularity spread like a benevolent virus so that now it seems there is not a street left untouched by the hand of Midas and at night, on Charles Bridge, even the silence bears his fingerprints. On the corner of Liliová and Karlova stands the Renaissance house **At the Golden Serpent** (U zlatého hada) which was home in 1714 to the owner of the first coffee house in Prague, the Armenian Deodatus Damajan. This was located in the **House at the Three Ostriches** (U tří pštrosů) next to Charles Bridge in the Malá Strana and would have provided valuable sustenance in the winter for those braving the bitter winds that course up the Vltava, peeling the surface of the river and turning the air-borne droplets to ice. The house, with its fine Renaissance murals and painted ceilings, now houses a restaurant and hotel. Karlova finishes its journey by skirting the walls of the Holy Saviour, the second church located within the precinct of the Clementinum, and opens out into the tiny square of the Crusader Knights (Křižnovicke náměstí). Today, however, the area feels less like a square than an extraordinarily picturesque crossroads, where the stream of vehicles using the somewhat intrusive embankment road battles constantly with the pedestrian traffic surging ever onwards towards Charles Bridge.

The area of the bridgehead on the Old Town side was settled in 1252 by the Czech order of the Knights of the Cross with a Red Star, who had previously been attached to the hospice associated with the Convent of the Blessed Agnes. Here they built a hospital in the crypt of the domed Baroque **Church of St. Francis**. This church, built by J.B Mathey between 1679 and 1689, exists almost as the faint echo of St. Nicholas in Malá Strana, whose larger dome sings out from the other side of the Vltava, beckoning the traveller across the wide waters like a benevolent Siren. Passing the statue of Charles IV, set up in 1848 to commemorate the 500th anniversary of the founding of Charles University, we enter the long afternoon shadow of the Old Town Bridge Tower. Begun in 1391, this magnificent defensive gateway guarding what was then the only crossing of the Vltava, was the work of Peter Parler and his cathedral workshop. Although the western, bridge facade was badly damaged by Swedish shelling in 1648, the east still bears witness to the exceptional quality of Bohemian Gothic sculpture. In the middle of the wall above the gateway, ranged with the heraldic shields of those lands that were at the time part of the Czech domains, are displayed a triumvirate of particular significance to the bridge.

Standing in the centre, atop a relief representation of two bridge arches, is the patron saint of the bridge, St. Vitus. On his right sits Charles IV wearing the Imperial crown while his son Wenceslas IV, responsible for the completion of the bridge, is enthroned to his left wearing the crown of a Roman King. The decorations once bore a grisly addition, however, when after the execution of the twenty-seven leaders of the anti-Habsburg rebellion, twelve of the rebels' heads were fixed to the Tower and remained there for ten years, from 1621 to 1631.

Charles Bridge, with its 520 meters of cobbled, pedestrian walkway, stretches like a stone carpet between the Old Town and the Malá Strana, the waters of the river splitting round each of its sixteen piers as if they were the petrified thighs of some stubborn and resolute ogre. The first bridge on this site was built in 1118, a little to the north of the present structure. This early wooden bridge was torn to pieces by flood waters in 1157 and replaced a year later by a new stone bridge, the second oldest in Europe after Regensburg, known eponymously as the Judith Bridge after King Vladislav II's second wife. The smaller of today's two Malá Strana bridge towers is in fact the original gateway to the earlier bridge, in whose interior is preserved one of the most important pieces of Prague Romanesque relief sculpture showing the King on his throne with what is probably a figure representing the builder of the bridge kneeling by his side. The Judith Bridge sustained the insistent onslaught of the Vltava for nearly two hundred years before it too was destroyed by flooding in 1342. The triumphant successor, started in 1357 by Peter Parler and completed in the early fifteenth century, has survived right down to the present day. Tradition has it that the mortar used in the construction had its binding power enhanced by the addition of eggs to the mix. Charles IV himself was rumoured to have appealed to his people to bring as many eggs as possible to the site, the story relating how the peasants from the countryside responded by arriving with cartloads — all of them unfortunately hardboiled! Whatever the secret of its longevity, the bridge remains one of the most majestic anywhere, affording a promenade guarded by ranks of statuary that are themselves subject to the permanent vigil of an almost endless spiral of gulls. This notion of an avenue of statues, borrowed from the Ponte Sant'Angelo in Rome, harnessed the skills of some of the best Baroque sculptors in Prague to steal these silent attendants from the roll of popular Czech hagiography. The oldest piece of sculpture on the bridge is the bronze crucifix by J. Hilger (1629), set in its place (third on the right from the Old Town Bridge Tower) in 1657. The incongruity of the Hebrew lettering set round the cross results from an incident in 1695, when a member of the Jewish community was ordered by the courts to install it by way of atoning for his abuse of Christ, who was naturally unable to sue for slander on his own behalf. This statue, together with that of St. John of Nepomuk (eighth on the right from the Old Town Bridge Tower) are the only two to be made of bronze. All the others, with the exception of that of St. Philip Benizi (third on the left from the Malá Strana bridge towers) which is marble, are fashioned from sandstone. Due to the softness of this stone a number of the originals have now been removed to the lapidarium of the State Museum, their place having been taken by copies. The figure of John of Nepomuk is a relatively recent addition to Catholic hagiography, having been canonized in 1729 as a symbol of revitalized Catholicism. But the reason for his canonization was based on an erroneous account of his martyrdom at the hands of Wenceslas IV in 1393. This relates how John of Pomuk, the Archbishop of Prague at the time, was tortured and thrown into the Vltava for not revealing the details of the Queen's confession to her husband.

Prague's first coffee house, the House at the Three Ostriches.

43

Charles Bridge. The Old Town Bridge Tower guards the entrance to the Old Town.

Following pages Charles Bridge. The particular atmosphere of the avenue of Saints.

*Charles Bridge. M. B.
Mandl: Statue of St. Philip
Benizi (1714).*

*J. Hilger's bronze Crucifix
(1629).*

Henceforth he was known as Nepomuk (ne means no in Czech) for
his refusal to submit to the will of the monarch, thereby commending
himself for subsequent canonization as a staunch upholder of
confessional rights. In fact he was martyred because he defended the
rights of the church against the encroachment of secular power.
Whether or not the adherence to the apocryphal version was a
deliberate avoidance of the truth is not clear; however it did
conveniently sidestep any reference to an issue which, in the early
eighteenth century, was becoming topical once more, namely the
balance of temporal power between the state and the church.

M. B. Braun: wooden statue
of St. Jude Taddens (1712).
National Gallery, Convent
of St. George.

View down the Vltava from Letná Hill.

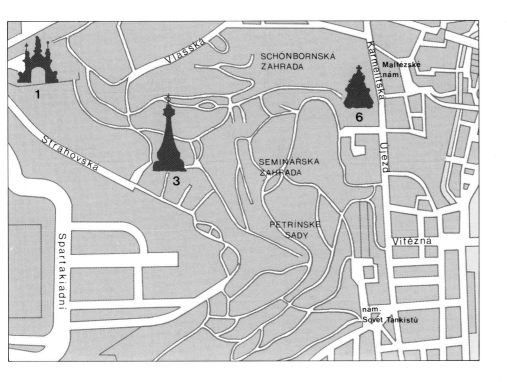

MALÁ STRANA

The area on the west bank of the Vltava, clinging to the banks
between the Letná and Petřín hills and climbing the slopes of the
Hradčany spur, is known as Malá Strana or Lesser Quarter. Like
much of the Old Town, it is dominated by the Baroque although
beneath that vestigial decoration the cores of many buildings are
much older. This was the second town of Prague, founded in 1257
by Přemysl Otakar II (1253-1278) with the aim of unifying the
scattered Romanesque settlements that had grown up in the castle's
shadow. However, this move was not meant to provide for his own
people, whom he moved out to a village nearby, instituting colonists
from Northern Germany in their place and thereby sowing the seeds
of nationalist friction which were to sprout and take root at various
periods in the future. In order to make the opportunity more
enticing they were offered assorted tax incentives and granted the
right to be governed by Magdeburg law.

At its foundation it was called the New Town (Nové Město) to
distinguish it from its slightly earlier counterpart across the river and
only became known as the Lesser Quarter with the establishment of
Charles IV's New Town in 1348. In its early days the area was not
really on an equal footing with the Old Town as it depended almost
entirely on the castle for its livelihood. Added to this, its
administrative powers were severely limited by the domination of the
territory by the two monastic orders of St. John and St. Thomas and
by the encroachment of the Old Town citizens who were laying claim
not only to the whole length of Charles Bridge but also to the banks
of Malá Strana and even the lower slopes of Petřín Hill.

During the building boom under Charles IV the boundaries of the

Left
*The dome of St. Nicholas
marks Malá Strana from
afar.*

53

The Hunger Wall glimpsed
through the trees that
surround the Church of St.
Lawrence on Petřín Hill.

quarter were extended considerably and outlying settlements which had previously been excluded from the protection of the Premyslid fortifications were encompassed by the new walls built around 1360. The section of this wall that runs up the southern end of the Petřín Hill is known as the **Hunger Wall** as it supposedly provided work for the town's builders at a time when starvation threatened, after a prolonged period of unemployment.

None of these fortifications, however, were able to protect the district from the destruction wrought by the rebellious Hussite citizens in the first quarter of the fifteenth century, when much of the area was laid waste in the course of their battles against the royal garrison stationed at Prague Castle.

It was to be the best part of fifty years before Malá Strana recovered architecturally from the devastation and even then the fabric of the town lasted only until 1541, when a merciless fire ravaged the whole quarter, its flames penetrating the castle complex and damaging the as yet incomplete St. Vitus Cathedral. Although it is unfortunate that so much of the original Gothic buildings were claimed by the conflagration, in a way it was a propitious event for the rooting of Renaissance architecture in Prague, providing as it did the opportunity for a widescale remodelling of the quarter.

That it occurred a mere fifteen years after the accession of the mighty Austrian Habsburgs to the throne of Bohemia meant that both the political motivation and the economic conditions were ideal for the restructuring of Malá Strana. Whole families of Italian craftsmen were imported to assist in the operation, many of them settling in and around the street Vlašská. Although the character of Malá Strana was largely modelled during the Baroque period, much of the underlying framework is the result of this Renaissance reconstruction.

The atmosphere one encounters on crossing into Malá Strana is quite distinct from that of the Old Town on the other side of the river. Despite the fact that it was founded as a commercial centre, operating from what still is the central focus — the **Lesser Quarter Square** (Malostranské náměstí) — Malá Strana really came into its own after the Battle of the White Mountain in 1620 when wealthy families loyal to the victorious Habsburgs settled in the area. Here they found large tracts of land abandoned by the members of the Bohemian nobility and burghers who had refused to adopt the Catholic faith and who had therefore been forced to emigrate.

The widespread availability of land and its proximity to the Castle, with whose scale and grandeur many of the remaining nobles sought to compete, provided the ideal circumstances for them to indulge in ambitious building projects and the laying out of magnificent summer gardens which, together with the green expanses of the Petřín and Letná Hills, imbue the surroundings with the quality of an aristocratic playground.

The proportions of the present square remain much as they were at the foundation of the Gothic town, although, as in the case of the Old Town Square, the Gothic cores of the buildings are hidden behind Renaissance and Baroque facades dating from subsequent redevelopments. The space is dominated by the massive presence of

Mostecká -
on the coronation route
to the Castle.

Right
The Church of St. Nicholas
dwarfs the other buildings
in the square.

the high Baroque **Church of St. Nicholas** (Chrám svatého Mikuláše) and the adjoining former Jesuit college. Together they divide the square into two, as indeed it had been from the outset when the central portion was occupied by the Gothic Church of St. Nicholas (founded in 1283), its attendant rectory and graveyard and a Romanesque rotunda of St. Wenceslas. In 1625, shortly after the Battle of the White Mountain, the Gothic church was donated to the Jesuits; over the following decades they built their college, the first of several in Prague, established to train the large number of clerics necessary for the reinstitution of Catholicism. It was not until 1704, however, that work was started on a church whose magnitude was in keeping with the scale of the mission of conversion on which the order had embarked. This new church was initiated by Christian Dientzenhofer, who built the basilica which forms the nave of the

church today. It was his son, however, Kilian Ignaz, who went on to extend the church by adding a sacristy surmounted by the great dome which, together with Lurago's finely proportioned belfry tower, has become the symbol not only of Malá Strana but also of the triumph of Catholicism and of its visual vehicle, the Baroque. The interior is no less impressive, with its vast ceiling fresco in the nave (1500 sq. metres) ranking as one of the largest paintings in Europe. It is the sheer scale of the details, such as the gargantuan statues of church teachers that guard the piers of the dome, which generates an atmosphere of restrained power, unlike some other Baroque interiors where the force is lost beneath a clutter of overweight decoration that excludes the light and roots the imagination to the floor, when it should be sent soaring vaultward. The first Baroque church to be built in Prague is situated in Malá Strana on Karmelitská. Ironically, bearing in mind that Baroque was the style of the Counter-Reformation, the church was built and consecrated to the Holy Trinity by the community of German Lutherans on the site of a former Hussite church. After the Battle of the White Mountain it was donated by the Emperor to the order of the bare-footed Carmelites, who rebuilt it and reconsecrated it to **St. Mary Victorious** (Kostel P. Marie Vítězné), thereby hinting at the bellicose strain of the Counter-Reformation and its positive missionary zeal. Inside is a rather unusual object of spiritual contemplation, a wax doll brought from Spain and donated to the church by Polyxena of Lobcowicz in 1628. This celebrated miniature mannequin, much like the one in the Church of Aracoeli in Rome, is dressed by nuns in ornately embroidered robes and precious jewels, votive gifts from noble Catholic ladies. He looks down from his extravagantly embellished display case on pilgrims from all over the world, who flock here to address their prayers to the doll in the hope that faith in his ability as a miracle worker is well founded. In the catacombs beneath the church, the bodies of Carmelite friars in a miraculous state of preservation would probably testify that it is. At the lower north east corner of the square stands the late Renaissance **Lesser Town Hall** (Malostranská radnice) which administered the cultural, political and economic affairs of Malá Strana until 1784, when the towns of Prague were unified and run as a single unit. Before this the heterogeneous character of the towns was mirrored by a corresponding diversity of religious belief which, since the beginning of the Hussite Wars, had split the population into clearly definable factions. These included offshoots of the original Utraquist reform movement, further diversified by their adhesion to the northern European Calvinist or Lutheran trends. Towards the end of the sixteenth century the division between the Catholic, monarchical autocracy of the Habsburgs and the Protestant Bohemian Estates had deepened, but the Estates still had considerable bargaining power at the Czech Diet, or Land Registry. When in 1575 Maximilian II sought the approval of the Estates to raise an extra levy for a campaign against the Turks in Hungary, along with acceptance of his son Rudolf as the future King, the Estates agreed on condition that he in return should grant tolerance to non-Catholics. Realizing that Ferdinand would try and exploit the internal division of the different arms of Protestantism, they strengthened the tenor of their

The Church of St. Mary Victorious.

The Church of St. Nicholas with Dientzenhofer's dome and Lurago's belfry. A synthesis of German and Italian influences results in the definitive Prague Baroque church.

demand by grouping under a common front and signing a concordat known as the Bohemian Confession, the terms of which were thrashed out here in the Lesser Town Hall. Although Maximilian's concessions were not as far reaching as might have been hoped and nothing was committed to writing for posterity, he did accept the existence of a Protestant establishment.

It was not until 1609, however, that the Protestant demands for religious freedom were granted by Rudolf II in his charter known as the Letter of Majesty, and then only because he required their support to counter the ambitions of his younger brother Matthias, who himself had designs on the Bohemian throne. The mood of tolerance and religious pluralism did not last long, however, and the perennial differences surfaced once more when, prompted by a clear violation of the terms of the charter by certain members of the government, the Estates convened and plotted the downfall of the errant ministers. This meeting took place in the late Renaissance **Smiřický Palace** (No. 18/6), which dominates the north-western corner of the square, on May 22nd 1618. And from this palace the next day a group of representatives departed for the castle to carry

The Waldstein garden.

out what became known as the Second Defenestration of Prague. Although no one was seriously injured, due to the fortuitous positioning of a pile of excrement and general refuse below the window from which they were thrown, this action lit the fuse for the Battle of the White Mountain, which in turn ignited the pan-European conflict of the Thirty Years War.

The whole northern end of the upper square is closed by the **Lichtenstein Palace** which takes its name from the notorious governor Karel of Lichtenstein. Known as the Bloody Governor for his remorseless persecution of the leaders of the anti-Habsburg uprising, he was ultimately responsible for the mass executions on the Old Town Square and the subsequent display of the heads on the Old Town Bridge Tower.

Leaving the square via Tomášská takes you in the direction of what is without doubt the grandest and most opulent of the Baroque palaces in Malá Strana — the Waldstein. As in the Old Town it is advisable to look up from time to time so as not to miss details on the facades of buildings that might otherwise go unnoticed. Set above an entrance (No. 4/26) about half way along Tomášská on the right, for example, is perhaps the most sculpturally ornate of Prague's house signs depicting St. Hubert and a stag, by F.M. Brokoff.

Shortly afterward the street opens up into Waldstein Square (Valdštejnské náměstí), the whole east side of which is taken up by the facade of the early Baroque palace of the same name. At first sight **Waldstein Palace**, despite its evident size, does not look like a building that could compete in scale and grandeur with the Castle complex on Hradčany; but one only has to follow its perimeter wall all the way along Valdštejnská, taking a right into Klárov and trace the return wall running up Letenská, to realize that the facade by comparison is but a humble apology for the embarrassment of riches. The man behind this imposing group of buildings, which is almost like a self-contained town, was the phenomenally successful and consequently enormously wealthy general, Albrecht of Wallenstein (1583-1634). Wallenstein had made his name and personal fortune as a condottiere in the service of Ferdinand II, rising to become the Imperial Generalissimo during the Thirty Years War. Having been awarded the title of Duke of Friedland, he profited greatly from the confiscation of property belonging to the Czech nobility in the wake of the Battle of the White Mountain, amassing the finances necessary to embark on his ambitious project in Malá Strana. His was to be the first of the mighty Baroque palaces that proliferate in the quarter, a palace which was composed of five interconnecting courtyards and a magnificent garden held in the embrace of rambling wings that spread almost to the foot of Letná Hill. Twenty-five houses and three private gardens were bought up and demolished to make way for the dynastic home which was to stay in the family right up until 1945. Although the interior now houses the Ministry of Education and is therefore inaccessible, the splendid Italianate garden is open during the spring and summer (entrance in Letenská). Designed and built exclusively by Italians, the Latin influence is nowhere more apparent than in the combination of statuary, artificial pools and grottoes ranged around the central axis deriving from the richly frescoed, triple-arched loggia. This was said to be the source of Wallenstein's greatest pride and understandably so, casting as it does its triocular gaze down the avenue of copies of bronze statues by Adrien de Vries, court sculptor to Emperor Rudolf II. The originals, like many of the art treasures that existed on this side of the river, were looted by the Swedes during the Thirty Years War and now reside in the grounds of Drottingholm Palace near Stockholm. The vast scale of Wallenstein's palace, which is best appreciated from the vantage point outside the lower east gate of the Castle, cocks an almost contemptuous snook at the residence of his Lord and Master high up on the Hradčany spur. Wallenstein, however, was a double dealer whose ambitions ultimately o'erleapt themselves. Not satisfied with the pre-eminent position he had won for himself in the Imperial court, he entered into clandestine negotiations with the opposing forces of the Protestant cause who were offering him the Bohemian crown in return for his support. Ferdinand II took no chances with Wallenstein's wavering allegiance, possibly recalling that he was in any case a convert to the Catholic fold, and had him murdered at Cheb (present-day Eger) in western Bohemia. Waldstein Palace was the first of many aristocratic residences that sprang up in Malá Strana, the stronghold of the predominantly German-speaking

Adrian De Vries: Hercules and the Golden Apples of the Hesperides. National Gallery, Convent of St. George.

Right
Waldstein Palace stucco and fresco work on the ceiling of the Sala Terrena.

nobility. Many of the streets and nearly all of the squares are littered with the palaces of powerful families such as the Lobcowicz, Kolowrat and Černín clans. On Valdštejnská alone there are four, perhaps most remarkable for their terraced gardens laid out on the slopes in the very shadow of the Castle. All of these, with the exception of the Fürstenberg garden which is the property of the Polish Embassy, are open to the public, access being gained by the entrance next to Kolowrat Palace (No.10/154).

The palaces no longer function as private residences, but thankfully they have been kept in use either as the offices of various Czech ministries or as the seats of foreign embassies. In fact Malá Strana is Prague's Embassy Land, the vast majority of them located in palaces in the streets Vlašská and Nerudova and in the tranquil Maltese (Maltézské) and Grand Priory (Velkopřevorské) squares. When there are no people around in these two pockets of untouched Baroque serenity it requires little imagination to transport oneself back to the days of frock coats and powdered wigs, of balls that Casanova himself attended, of gauntlets thrown down to the intricate lilt of chamber music and of scores settled at dawn while the mists from the Vltava still clung between the cobbles. Tycho de Brahe, Rudolf's astronomer, sacrificed his nose in one such duel, thereafter sporting a silver proboscis to hide his loss of face. **Maltese Square** takes its name from the Monastery of the Order of St. John, or Maltese Knights, who settled and fortified the bridgehead of the old Judith Bridge in 1169. The **Church of Our Lady Below the Chain** (Kostel Panny Marie pod řetězem) in Lázeňská formed the heart of the monastic buildings. Although the original Romanesque building was subject to an extensive Gothic reconstruction in the mid-fourteenth century, elements of the earlier structure are preserved in the courtyard of the present church behind the large prismatic towers which front the street. On the corner on the left where Lázeňská enters Grand Priory Square, is the Baroque palace of the same name (No.4/485) which now serves as the Museum of Czech Music and houses a fascinating collection of old musical instruments along with the musical archives of the National Museum. Further down the square, which is closed on the southern side by the French Embassy in the **Buquoy Palace**, there is a monument to a more recent brand of musical hero. On a stretch of wall, which under the Communists saw the frequent posting of guards to counter anti-establishment graffiti, Prague has its own John Lennon memorial next to images drawn from The Beatles along with slogans committed to the idea of freedom of speech. At the far end of the square a little bridge spans the branch of the river known as Čertovka and leads onto **Kampa Island**. Čertovka, which translates as The Devil's Stream, probably takes its name from an eccentric woman who lived in the house At the Seven Devils (U sedmi čertů) in Maltese Square. The island provides ideal respite from the crowds thronging over Charles Bridge and up to the Castle, as well as offering an unforgettable panorama of the bridge and the embankments of the Old Town running down towards the National Theatre with its roof crowned with gilded railings and glinting in the sun. In earlier days the blaze of colourful pageant that accompanied the coronation procession could be seen

PALLANTES

ENEAS

"Prague Venice."

Right
House signs in Malá Strana.

passing over Charles Bridge, up Mostecká, through the Lesser Town Square and, with horses breaking into a sweat, into the long climb of Nerudova. Yet more of the characteristic house signs proliferate along Nerudova as well as the straining, Baroque stone figures that support the portals and windows of palaces, such as the blackamoors set into the facade of **Morzin Palace**, or the eagles guarding the entrance to the Italian Embassy. At the top of Nerudova you can either follow the road round into Ke Hradu which brings you out in front of the castle; or take the steps (Radnické schody) up into the western end of Hradčany Square.

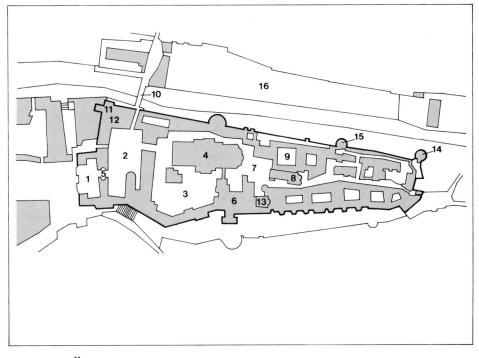

1. First Courtyard
2. Second Courtyard
3. Third Courtyard
4. St. Vitus Cathedral
5. Matthias Gateway
6. Royal Palace
7. St. George Square
8. Basilica of St. George
9. Convent of St. George
10. Powder Bridge
11. Spanish Hall
12. Gallery
13. All Saints' Church
14. Dalibor's Tower
15. White Tower
16. Gardens

HRADČANY CASTLE

The castle spreads its massive wings like a huge bird of prey hovering above Malá Strana on the west bank of the Vltava at the old fording point of the ancient east-west trade route. Legend has it that the mythical Princess Libuše, renowned for her prophetic powers, foresaw the great destiny in store for Prague. Perched high atop her residence at Holy Vyšehrad she surveyed the forested slopes of the opposite bank, declaring in an oracular voice, "I can see a vast city whose fame reaches to the stars." Then she sent her followers into the forest with instructions to found a town at the point where they saw a ploughman called Přemysl building the threshold (prah) of a house. Hence the title of the dynasty — the Premyslids — and the name of the city — Praha. According to some chroniclers these mythical origins date from the eighth century. But archaeological evidence dates the construction of the first castle at the second half of the ninth century, when Duke Bořivoj, having conquered the Czech tribes who had settled below the escarpment, resolved to fortify it.

Attempting the summit of Hradčany via the precipitous streets of Nerudova and Vlašská, it is immediately apparent just why the Castle is so well sited. Initially, however, the Castle was no more than a wooden hilltop fort with earthen ramparts. It was not until the eleventh century, during the reign of Břetislav I, that these were replaced with a stone curtain wall two metres thick and further fortified with two towers at the east and west ends. One hundred years later much of the present layout of the Castle complex was determined by the building programme of Soběslav I (1125-1140), although he himself continued to reside upriver at Vyšehrad (High Castle).

In 1303 the Castle was gutted by fire and left deserted until 1333, when Charles IV ordered its reconstruction during the reign of his

Prague Castle - part of the unmistakable skyline.

"I can see a vast city whose fame reaches to the stars."

67

Battling giants atop the gates to the First Courtyard.

The Castle gates.

father John of Luxemburg. Under Charles Prague was to become, with the extension of Malá Strana and the foundation of the New Town, the largest and most important city in Central Europe. Charles was one of the first of the highly erudite mediaeval European rulers. Educated in Paris by the later to be Pope Clement VII and married to a French princess, his contact with the cultural hub of Western Europe and his favourable relations with the Holy See, which was then in Avignon and dominated by the French, had far reaching effects on the growth of the city, both politically and artistically. His reconstruction of the Castle modelled itself after the designs of the great Gothic palaces in Paris, providing him not only with an elegant residence but also a potent symbol of Prague's elevated status in international affairs. Part of these palace buildings are preserved beneath the Vladislav Hall but, like much of the previous and subsequent structural developments, they were enshrouded by the large-scale but rather uninspiring Neo-Classical reconstruction commissioned during the eighteenth century by Empress Maria Theresa.

The present Castle is laid out around three interconnecting courtyards, the first of which opens onto Hradčany Square. This courtyard with its wrought iron, Rococo gates was built on top of the castle moat during the eighteenth-century redevelopment and provides the scene every day at midday for the changing of the palace guard. This used to be a solemn, grey, goose-stepping affair but now, aided by the splash of colour provided by the new uniforms commissioned from Theodor Pištěk (the Oscar winning costume

designer for *Amadeus*, which was shot here in Prague), the young conscripts seem in an embarrassed sort of way to enjoy it as much as the crowds of onlookers. From the tops of the gate piers copies of statues by I. F. Platzer (1768), muscle bound, battling giants look down in a swirl of motionless stone on the stock still guards who are petrified by comparison.

Crossing the first courtyard we come to the stolid **Matthias Gate**, its rough hewn face imprisoned by the pale skinned embrace of the wings of Maria Theresa's palace. This gateway, built by Emperor Matthias in 1614, was the first secular Baroque structure, providing a free standing western entrance to the Castle before it was incorporated in the eighteenth-century redevelopment. The austerity of the second courtyard acts as a sort of airlock before entering the rarified atmosphere of the ancient core of the Castle grouped in and around the third. A northern entrance which opens to our left affords access, via the **Powder Bridge** (Prašný Most) spanning the Deer Pit, to the late Renaissance buildings of the **Riding School** and **Lion's Den** at one end of the **Summer Garden** (open only in spring). Laid out in 1534, this was one of the first gardens in the Italian style north of the Alps. Although the design of the garden has changed since then, its original ambience is maintained by the buildings of the **Ball Games Court** (Míčovna), built in Palladian style by the court architect Bonifaz Wolmut and Ulrico Aostalis in 1567-69, and the magnificent **Summer Palace of Queen Anne**. This building, arguably the most beautiful Renaissance building north of the Alps, with its unusual but elegant roof truss, like the upturned

Prague Castle: guards in new uniforms.

The Summer Palace of Queen Anne. The Italian architectural Renaissance arrives in Prague.

69

The remarkable "Singing Fountain."

"Singing Fountain," detail.

hull of a ship, was built between 1538 and 1563 at the behest of Emperor Ferdinand I (1526-1564), the first Habsburg to accede to the Bohemian throne. In effect this was the first building in Prague to be conceived from the outset in the spirit of the Italian Renaissance, giving impetus after the catastrophic fire of 1541 to other Bohemian noblemen for the construction of the Renaissance palaces which line Hradčany Square. Emperor Rudolf II (1576-1611) preferred to hold court here in the Summer Palace, listening to the haphazard voice of water on bronze produced by the **Singing Fountain** outside and maintaining the real world of politics and government at arm's length in the palace buildings on the other side of the Deer Pit. Rudolf it was that transformed the Castle of his day into a private museum to rival any in Europe, extending the castle along the northern wall of the second courtyard to house his remarkable collection, including works by Titian, Tintoretto, Veronese and Rubens as well as representative examples of Bohemian Baroque. But those that remain now, after the Swedish looting

during the Thirty Years War and the German looting during the occupation, are a pale shadow of the wonders with which Rudolf surrounded himself in his lifetime. Then the collection was bolstered by the presence of masterpieces of both the southern and northern Renaissance including paintings by Michelangelo, Leonardo Da Vinci, Raphael, Giorgione, Dürer, Holbein, Cranach and Brueghel. Some of these are preserved in the National Gallery's collection in the Sternberg Palace, but all together they represent only a fraction of Rudolf's patronage and compulsive desire to collect. In 1619 an inventory revealed that the collection ran to some three thousand paintings and two and a half thousand sculptures and was valued at the staggering sum of seventeen million guilders. Neither was this compulsion limited to the field of the figurative arts, taking in as it did clocks, scientific apparatus and a bizarre range of relics and natural curiosities including what purported to be the nails from Noah's Ark and a phial of the dust from which God created Adam. The name of Rudolf is synonymous with the flowering of the

St. Vitus from Nový Svět.

Renaissance in Prague, at a time when many wealthy rulers were turning away from the problems agitating in the social structure in favour of pursuits that examined the outer rather than the inner world. Rudolf was a solitary, mentally unstable depressive who preferred to devote his attentions to the host of alchemists he had brought to the city in his quest for the Philosopher's Stone (including the English magician Edgar Kelley), or to the astronomers scouring the heavens for clues to the order of the universe. In this he bore a remarkable similarity to another phenomenally wealthy late Renaissance patron in the same period in Florence, Francesco de' Medici, perhaps revealing the confusion that the prolonged questioning of the Renaissance had wrought in the minds of those closest to its heart.

The area now taken up by the Third Courtyard was the centre of the first settlement on the Hradčany spur. Much of the remnants from the earlier building developments have been consumed by Picassi's eighteenth-century redevelopment for Empress Maria Theresa which now contain State Rooms and presidential offices. The western and southern wings, for example, have as their core the original Romanesque fortifications erected by Soběslav I in the second quarter of the twelfth century and the lowest floor of the Old Royal Palace still contains the mighty barrel vaulting of the Soběslav Hall. The square is dominated, however, by the soaring presence of **St. Vitus Cathedral**, which commands the skyline for miles lifted aloft by

Left
The east end of St. Vitus with its fan of ambulatory chapels.

the powerful shoulders of the precipitous rocky outcrop of the Hradčany. The first church on this particular site, the Romanesque **Rotunda of St. Vitus**, was founded around 926 by Prince Wenceslas who, with his martyrdom at the hands of his brother Boleslav the Cruel in 935, was made patron saint of Bohemia and protector of the whole Czech nation. Initially intended to serve the needs of the Premyslid princes, it became the seat of Prague's bishops when the town was raised to a bishopric in 973. It was not long before the small rotunda had to be enlarged to serve the needs of a burgeoning royal community and in 1060, instigated by Prince Spytihněv II (1055-1061), building started on a new triple naved basilica. Remnants from the excavations of these two early structures are preserved in the antechambers of the Royal Burial Vault which may be entered via the staircase in the Chapel of the Holy Cross. When Charles IV succeeded in raising the status of Prague to an archbishopric in 1344, he founded the Cathedral of St. Vitus, summoning the French architect Mathieu d'Arras to plan and initiate the project. By the time of his death in 1352, Arras had completed only the choir ambulatory with its eight polygonal chapels, and it was

St. Vitus: the tympanum of the West Door.

St. Vitus: the West Door.

left to the innovatory genius of Peter Parler of Gmund to continue the work, reshaping the original designs with his own keen instinct for the principles of late Gothic architecture. He modified the polygonal chapels into square ones, enlarged the Chapel of St. Wenceslas and made of it a unit separate from that of the choir proper. His also is the design of the south transept and tower along with the main southern portal, known as the Golden Gate from the red and gold ground of the mosaic of the Last Judgement set into the facade. This elaborate representation, the work of a team of Italian mosaicists working around 1370, depicts the patron saints of Bohemia grouped beneath the central figure of Christ enthroned. Kneeling below in the spandrels of the central arch, hands clasped in solemn supplication, are the figures of Charles IV himself with his consort Elizabeth of Pomerania. By 1385 the east end of the Cathedral was completed and Parler's sons finished off the main steeple to the height of the later Renaissance parapet before 1406. Thereafter the best part of five hundred years were to pass before any major advances in the construction process were made. The Hussite Wars brought a halt to the westerly development of the

cathedral and the Neo-Gothic nave, the west facade and the west steeples were not completed until the end of the nineteenth century. The interior, however, does not hark of any great hiatus, the restrained Neo-Gothic nave directing the attention forward to the altar and the powerful contrast between the shade of the ambulatory arcades and the resplendent flood of light through the clerestory. This is not meant to detract from the quality of the nave, whose tardy addition allowed some of the greatest of Prague's nineteenth-century artists and glass craftsmen to collaborate on the strikingly beautiful scheme of stained and painted glass windows, through which the light throws myriad shafts, dappling the paving slabs with limpid colour. The most beautiful of these is the extraordinary Art Nouveau window (third chapel on the left from the West Door), depicting scenes from the lives of Saints Cyril and Methodius, by Alfons Mucha. Although Mucha was born in Prague, he spent much of his time in Paris where he was perhaps best known for his series of posters of Sarah Bernhardt.

Of all the Gothic chapels set around the east end and choir, by far the most venerated is that of **St. Wenceslas**. Richly adorned with

St. Vitus: view along the nave.

Page 78
Construction work on St. Vitus started here at the east end.

Page 79
St. Vitus: Alfons Mucha's stunning painted window in the New Archbishop's Chapel.

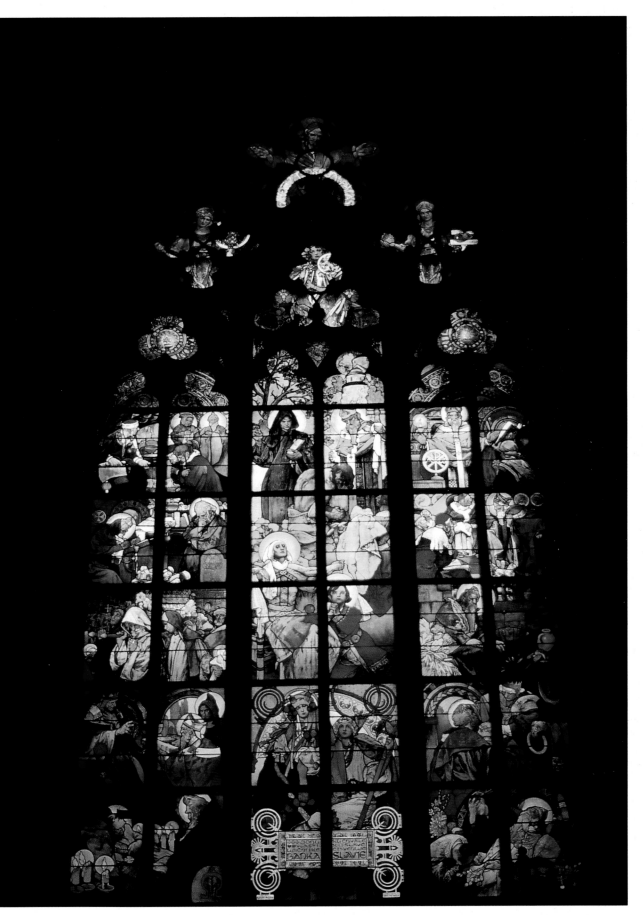

Gothic murals and inlaid with precious stones set into gold plaster in the Byzantine tradition, it is both an embodiment of the convergence of the eastern and western arms of Christianity and a tribute to the dominance of the latter under the guidance of Bohemia's most popular saint. A copy of the lion's head door ring to which Wenceslas clung while his brother Boleslav laid on mercilessly with his sword is attached to the door of the chapel.

Opposite the monument of Count Schlick, to the right of the choir, is the Chapel of the Holy Cross which gives access to the **Royal Burial Vault**. Here, enshrouded in granite and pewter sarcophagi, are preserved the remains of some of the Luxemburg dynasty of kings, including Charles IV and his son Wenceslas, along with those of the Habsburgs who made Prague their royal residence, Rudolf II and Maria Theresa. The exit brings us out in front of the late Renaissance white marble **Imperial Mausoleum**, bearing reliefs on the upper panel of Emperor Ferdinand I, his consort Anna Jagiello and his son Maximilian. On the lateral panels are depicted portraits of Charles IV and his four wives together with those of George of Poděbrady and Ladislav Posthumous. The sculptural decoration of the ground floor was devoted in the first instance to the past history of the Premyslid kings, the chapels bearing six tombs of Premyslid rulers. The triforium, however, is composed of twenty-one portrait busts, not only of members of the Luxemburg dynasty but also of Prague archbishops, the Master of Works and the two architects of the Gothic part of the Cathedral. The fact that commoners are presented alongside royalty and high ranking members of the clergy points towards the cult of the individual that was to become such an important precept of humanism and the Renaissance.

On either side of the high altar are positioned two wooden relief

carvings, by K. Bendl, from the first quarter of the seventeenth century. Looking towards the east end, the one on the left of the high altar depicts the Flight of the Winter King, Frederick V of the Palatinate after the Battle of the White Mountain. With its view of the Old Town, Charles Bridge and Malá Strana it provides an interesting architectural record of the city before the calamities of the Thirty Years War. When Emperor Matthias died in the spring of 1619 he should have been succeeded by his nephew Ferdinand Habsburg. The Protestant Bohemian Estates had other ideas, however, and rejected him in favour of Frederick, who they saw as a Protestant sympathiser. They had good reason to believe that Frederick would aid them in their cause, firstly because of his position at the head of the Union of German Protestants and secondly because of his marriage to Elizabeth, daughter of the English King James I, a vehement anti-Catholic. Frederick unfortunately proved to be weak and ineffectual, his reign lasting but a year before the snubbed Ferdinand, at the head of the joint armies of Bavaria and Saxony, returned to defeat the Bohemian Estates at the Battle of the White Mountain in 1620.

St. Wenceslas Chapel.

81

George and Martin of Cluj: St. George and the Dragon (1373). The earliest piece of free-standing bronze sculpture in Central Europe. National Gallery, St. George Convent.

Detail from the silver Tomb of St. John Nepomuk.

The Bohemian Chancellery, site of the Second Defenestration of Prague in 1618.

On the right of the High Altar, just beyond the second wooden relief panel which depicts a view of the city from about 1630, is the sumptuously wrought silver **Tomb of St. John of Nepomuk**. This exuberant and costly tomb, made in Vienna in 1733-36, reflects just how important the ubiquitous figure of the recently canonized saint was for the cause of the Catholic monarchic autocracy.

Outside, positioned roughly in the centre of the third courtyard, is a copy of a statue representing another saint who played a prominent part in the Czech hagiography, especially up here in the Castle precinct. Although sections of it were recast at the end of the sixteenth century, the statue of St. George and the Dragon (the original forms part of the National Gallery's collection installed nearby in the Convent of St. George) by George and Martin of Cluj is the oldest piece of free-standing Gothic bronze sculpture in Central Europe.

Beyond this, at the east end of the square, a small flight of steps leads up to the entrance to the **Old Royal Palace**. Deep in its bowels are preserved chambers from some of the earliest construction periods of the original fortifications, including the Soběslav Palace and parts of the ninth-century curtain walls. The central focus on this level, however, is provided by the enormous expanse of the **Vladislav Hall**, which at sixty-two metres in length, sixteen metres in width and rising to a height of thirteen metres, is by far the largest secular interior from this period in Prague. With its noble proportions and the intricacies of the reticulated Lierne vaulting it also ranks as one of the most beautiful. Built by Benedikt Ried between 1493 and 1503, it was here that the Bohemian kings were elected, and the walls once rang with the sound of hooves at the gallop when tournaments were actually held inside the palace. A special **Riders'**

Staircase, entering the Hall about two thirds along the left hand wall, was incorporated into the design for this very purpose. In the southwest corner of the Hall is the entrance to the chambers of the **Bohemian Chancellery**, the outermost of which was the scene of the Second Defenestration in 1618, when three aberrant governors were thrown out of the east window. Looking out of this window for a moment towards the exterior wall of the Vladislav Hall, the earliest elements of the Italian Renaissance to be incorporated in the architecture of Prague are visible in the rectangular, pilastered window linings that adorn the facade. At the east end of the Hall a flight of steps leads up into the oratory of **All Saints Chapel**, an earlier structure (1370-87) by Peter Parler, built to service the needs of the convent for noble ladies which was sited to the east of the Old Royal Palace. Also included amongst the chambers that open off the Vladislav Hall are the late Gothic **Hall of the Diet** in the northeast corner, and the **New Appeal Court** to the west of the Riders' Staircase, which exits onto St. George's Square. This is undoubtedly one of the most picturesque areas contained within the Castle walls. Borded to the south by the walls of the Church of All Saints and those of the Vladislav Hall, the space is presided over by the magisterial, russet facade of the **Basilica of St. George**. This church, apart from being the oldest in Hradčany, is the best

Following page
The imposing interior of Vladislav's Great Hall in the Old Royal Palace.

The Baroque façade of St. George's Church. The oldest surviving church in Prague.

Left
The early Romanesque interior of the Church of St. George.

Master Theodoric: St. Jerome (before 1365). National Gallery, Convent of St. George.

preserved example of Romanesque architecture not only in Prague but also in the whole of Bohemia. The facade is Baroque but the white towers that rise behind with their double orders of Romanesque arches beckon us to explore further. The church was founded as early as 912 by Duke Vratislav I, giving rise to the establishment of the adjacent convent, the first in Bohemia, in 937. The east towers were added after a fire in 1142 and shortly afterwards the lower part of the Chapel of St. Ludmila (Wenceslas's grandmother) was built on to the south tower. The church was further modified towards the end of the seventeenth century when it was given its present facade, but thanks to extensive archaeological research followed by a reconstruction programme the church has now had its original Romanesque appearance faithfully restored. The neighbouring convent contains a permanent exhibition of trends in Bohemian painting from the Gothic through to the Baroque. Exceptional amongst these are the bold portraits by Master Theodoric and the Crucifixion scenes by other masters whose names are not known, which reveal the persistent fascination with the Blood

Fourteenth century Bohemian Master: St. Vitus Madonna and Child. National Gallery, Convent of St. George.

Karel Skreta: Portrait of the gem cutter Dionysio Miseroni and family (1653). National Gallery, Convent of St. George.

Master of the Třebon Altar: Resurrection (before 1380). National Gallery, Convent of St. George.

Master of the Rajhrad Altar: Crucifixion (before 1420). National Gallery, Convent of St. George.

N° 22 Golden Lane: Franz Kafka lived and worked here. The Golden Lane at Prague Castle.

of Christ that was to prove central to the divergence of the Utraquists from the liturgy of the Roman Catholic Church.

Any tour of Hradčany should include a visit to the tiny street of fairytale houses known as the **Golden Lane** (Zlatá ulička), which line the northern wall of the castle beyond the east end of the Basilica of St. George. Legend has it that this is where Rudolf II installed his band of alchemists, but in fact it is now known that their workshops and laboratories were housed in the **Mihulkar Powder Tower** on Vikářská, where there is now an exhibition of some of the equipment they used in their experiments. These miniature houses were actually built by members of the palace guard who plied various trades at times when their armed services were not required. Today they are occupied on the whole by gift shops.

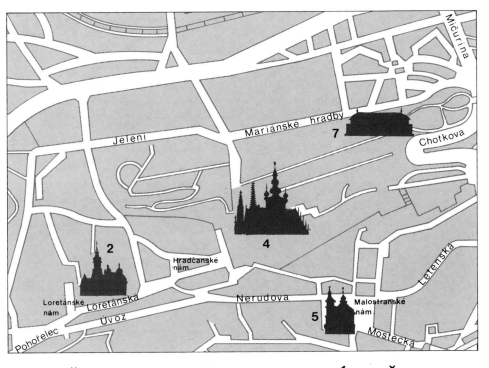

HRADČANY SQUARE AND NOVÝ SVĚT

In 1320 a third Prague settlement was founded by the Castle's burgrave, Berka of Duba. Originally intended as a town for serfs, its buildings were laid out on a site taking up about half the area of the present Hradčany Square. During the fourteenth century the town was considerably extended by Charles IV to include the areas of Úvoz, Pohořelec and Nový Svět, thereby filling in the gap between the Hradčany fortifications and those of the Strahov Monastery. However, despite its scale, the town was denied municipal independence for over two hundred and fifty years and therefore, due to its complete dependence on the castle, was considerably less important than either Malá Strana or the Old Town. The great fire which raged in Malá Strana and Hradčany in 1541 decimated the area, leaving the way clear for those nobles who wished to enhance their status and bring it to the attention of the neighbouring royals to develop Hradčany Square and skirt it with the large palaces which remain to the present day. The first of these was the **Schwarzenberg Palace** on the south side which now commands the top of Nerudova, its massive walls scored with diamond sgraffito in the style of the Italian Renaissance. On the opposite side of the square stands the later Baroque **Palace of the Archbishops of Prague** which, to the consternation of some tourists, completely conceals the buildings of the **Sternberg Palace**, now housing collections from the National Gallery of Prague. Access to this palace and its galleries may be gained through the unassuming arch on the far left of the facade of the Archbishop's Palace.

Leaving the square to the west via Kanovnická takes us past the beautiful **Martinic Palace** (No. 8/67), once more delicately adorned with sgraffito scenes from the Bible including King David and the Flight of Joseph from Potiphar. This narrow street, following the

*The magnificent
Schwarzenberg Palace.*

*Right
Albrecht Dürer: Feast of
the Rose Garlands (1506).
National Gallery, Sternberg
Palace.*

*Lucas Cranach the Elder:
Virgin and Child with
Saints Catherine and
Barbara (1510-1520).
National Gallery, Sternberg
Palace.*

The Archbishop's Palace.

natural lines of the hillocks beyond Hradčany and struck through
with a timeless, serene peace, runs into **Nový Svět** (New World), the
heart of the former poor quarter. Although it is known that Dvořák's
New World symphony was inspired by a trip to the United States,
the sleepy solitude of these streets is immediately redolent of its
mournful, long-suffering but stately theme. Taking a left into
Černínská at the end of Nový Svět leads us up into Loreto
Square, the scene of an unequal duel between the daunting, diamond
rusticated bulk of the **Černín Palace** and the peaceable centre of
pilgrimage opposite, the **Loreto**, armed only with the exquisite peal
of bells from her late seventeenth-century carillon. Behind K. I.
Dientzenhofer's Baroque facade is encircled the Santa Casa Shrine,
modelled on the one at Loreto in Italy, which according to the
legend was the house of the Virgin Mary, transferred there from the
Holy Land. About fifty of these shrines were built in Bohemia, as
part of the concerted attempt by the Counter-Reformation to
enhance the appeal of Catholicism to ordinary people. But they were
also popular amongst the pilgrims of the nobility who made precious
votive offerings of quite extraordinary value, including the renowned

Left
The tranquility of Nový Svět.

Martinic Palace.

The imposing façade of the Černín Palace.

Loreto: The Clock Tower with its seventeenth-century carillon.

Entrance to the Loreto and its Santa Casa shrine.

Left
The garden façade of
Černín Palace.

Diamond Monstrance, from the Loreto Treasury.

Right
The spires of Strahov from the Castle ramp.

Diamond Monstrance (c. 1699, Vienna), exhibited upstairs in the Loreto Treasury.

Pohořelec runs west from the far end of the square towards the **Strahov Monastery** whose twin spires topped with onion domes dominate the northern slopes of Petřín Hill. Founded in 1140 by Vladislav II, it is the oldest Premonstratensian monastery in Bohemia and was originally fortified because until the construction of the Hunger Wall in about 1320, it lay outside the fortifications of Hradčany. Here, over the centuries, the brothers amassed a staggering quantity of illustrated manuscripts and books so that by the end of the eighteenth century the collection included volumes

Strahov Monastery:
The Philosophical Hall.

containing very nearly the entire literary output of western Christianity. Small wonder then that when the Czech State dissolved all religious orders in Czechoslovakia in 1952, incorporating their collections into the monastery library, they had in the Strahov a ready-made Museum of National Literature, which is the purpose it serves today. The Old Library, which even before the dissolution

*Strahov Monastery:
the Theological Hall.*

contained in the region of 130,000 volumes, now comprises a
mammoth 900,000 books, as well as 5,000 illuminated manuscripts.
However, the central focus of its exhibition is formed by the
collections installed in the **Theological Hall** and the adjacent
Philosophical Hall, situated in the building to the right of the Baroque
Church of the Assumption (Kostel Nanebevzetí Panny Marie).

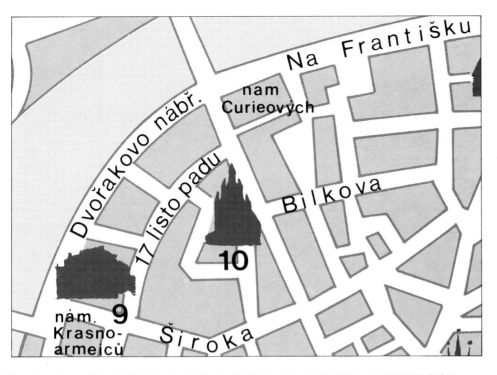

JOSEFOV, THE FORMER PRAGUE GHETTO

The Jews were early settlers in Prague. Ever vigilant for those areas likely to reap the profits of international trade, they were among the first aliens to realize the rich future that Prague had in store, due to its position on the main east-west trade route. Their original communities sprang up around the beginning of the tenth century in the Malá Strana, in the area now known as Újezd, and beneath the Vyšehrad on the opposite bank of the Vltava. During the thirteenth century there was a gradual expansion from these early settlements into the vicinity of the present-day Old New Synagogue. The Jews that populated the narrow winding alleys between the Old Town Square and the bend of the Vltava were segregated from the Christian community not only by the philosophical differences of their creed, but also by the physical barrier of a wall. This had been built in accordance with the edict of the Third Lateran Council (1179), which stated that areas inhabited by Jews should be separated from the dwellings of Christians by a fence, wall or moat.
In the first instance, therefore, the term Jewish Town indicated not the administrative autonomy of the area, but rather the first step towards the ghettoizing process of the sixteenth century, when any incoming Jews were compulsorily settled in the district. This ghetto underwent a significant expansion during the seventeenth century so that by the time of the Habsburg Kings Maximilian and Rudolf II, there were probably as many as seven thousand Jews packed into what must have become a network of narrow, squalid and unhygienic lanes. The conditions became so horrendous that even the distracted Rudolf lent an ear to the proposals of his finance minister Mordechaj Markus Maisl, who subsequently arranged for the repaving of the ghetto, the construction of the Jewish Town Hall and the Maisl Synagogue, and established the Old Jewish cemetery. Maislova, the

Left
The Jewish Town Hall and the Old New Synagogue.

103

*Preceeding pages
The Old New Synagogue.*

*The Old New Synagogue
and the monument to
Moses.*

street in which the eponymous Synagogue stands, was named in memory of his philanthropic redevelopment.

Much of the old Jewish Town was demolished during slum clearances at the end of the nineteenth century when the new buildings were laid out around the straight and largely characterless street of Pařížská. However, the core buildings of the religious community were preserved even through the Nazi occupation, when Hitler had intended to found a museum to an extinct race here in Prague. Some of the artefacts that he collected from synagogues all over Europe for that very purpose are preserved here in the buildings of the Jewish State Museum.

About three quarters of the way up Pařížská, on the left, we come to the **Old New Synagogue**. (Tickets for all the exhibitions of the Jewish State Museum may be purchased from the High Synagogue, opposite the entrance to the Old New Synagogue in Červená).

The Old New Synagogue is one of the first Gothic structures in Prague. The oldest part dates back to the mid-thirteenth century, making it the oldest preserved synagogue in Europe. Originally consisting only of a barrel vaulted lower chamber, the building was enlarged by the construction of a double aisled hall in the last quarter of the century, thereby creating the space necessary to hold separate services for men and women. The only time when Jewish men and women are permitted to worship together is during the wedding ceremony. The proportions and decoration inside are governed by the number twelve, symbolizing the twelve tribes of Israel. The benches lining the walls are late Empire and are still used in the services today. There is one seat, however, that no one is allowed to use. This is due to the fact that this seat, situated to the right of the altar, belonged to the legendary Rabbi Löwe.

Rabbi Löwe was a leading figure in the Jewish community during the reign of Rudolf II, best remembered now for his association with the ancient mystical creature — the Golem. Legend has it that he created the Golem in the dead of night from the clay and mud on the banks of the Vltava. The creature would lie dormant until the Shem (a Hebrew magic word) was uttered and the sign of life was placed in his mouth. With that the Golem was animated and became charged with the mission of going out into the community, discovering crimes and preventing them. Perhaps it was the Golem that persuaded Rudolf to do something about the appalling conditions in the ghetto. All went well until one evening before the Sabbath when Rabbi Löwe forgot to remove the sign of life from the mouth of the Golem. Even mythical monsters need a day off and the creature thus denied fell into an orgy of destruction in the Rabbi's house. The Rabbi, alerted by the commotion, found the Golem, deactivated him by chanting another Shem and then removed the sign of life from the creature's mouth. With this, the monster turned back into clay and mud and was finally laid to rest beneath the roof timbers of the Old New Synagogue.

On the corner of Červená and Maislova is situated the **Jewish Town Hall**, built in the late sixteenth century with funding from Mayor M. Maisl as an administrative centre. Although this recognized a certain degree of autonomy, it was not until 1850 that the Jewish Town

The Neo-Romanesque cemetery house.

became a separate quarter of the city and was renamed Josefov in memory of Emperor Joseph II. Crossing over Maislova, head down the street called U starého hřbitova towards the Neo-Romanesque turreted building which guards the entrance to the Old Jewish Cemetery. On the left as the street bends sharply to the right is the **Klaus Synagogue**, housing an exhibition of Hebrew manuscripts and old prints, including one of Tycho de Brahe with his silver nose. The building to the right of the entrance to the **Old Jewish Cemetery** houses a rather harrowing display of drawings by the children of Terezín concentration camp.

The cemetery is one of the most bizarre and stirring sights in Prague. There are over ten thousand bodies piled one on top of the other here, beneath the grey disarray of tombstones which lean toward the ground like teeth rocking in decaying gums. Coffins were not used, the bodies being simply wrapped in muslin, thereby facilitating the stacking process. Small pebbles placed in rows along every available edge of the stones supplant the Christian tradition of adorning graves with flowers. Also unlike Christian practice, where one tombstone

Gravestones in the Old Jewish Cemetery.

might mark the resting place of a whole family, here there is a separate stone for every person, except for children under the age of one. Among the celebrated figures of the Jewish community buried here are Jehuda Ben Bezalel, the famous Rabbi Löwe, Mordechaj Maisl, the mayor of the Jewish town, the physician and physicist, Josef Delmedigo, and the connoisseur of the Talmud David Oppenheimer. The stones are inscribed with symbols that relate to the name or profession of the deceased. The grave of Rabbi Löwe, for example, bears the symbol of the lion, which is the meaning of his surname in German. Alternatively, the symbol of crossed hands is reserved for those with connections with priestly or Levite families. An aristocratic coat-of-arms is to be found on the gravestone of Hindel Basevi, recalling the fact that she was the wife of the first Prague Jew to be raised to the nobility. Through the trees to the south-west sits the Gothic, single-naved Pinkas Synagogue which now serves as a memorial to the 77,297 Bohemian and Moravian Jews who lost their lives in the Nazi gas chambers. Their names, 36,000 of them relating to former citizens of Prague, are inscribed on the walls of the interior.

Jewish gravestones often portrayed a symbol relating either to the name or the profession of the deceased.

*The wall in the Pinkas
Synagogue bearing the
names of those Jews who
perished in Nazi
concentration camps.*

The tomb of Rabbi Löwe.

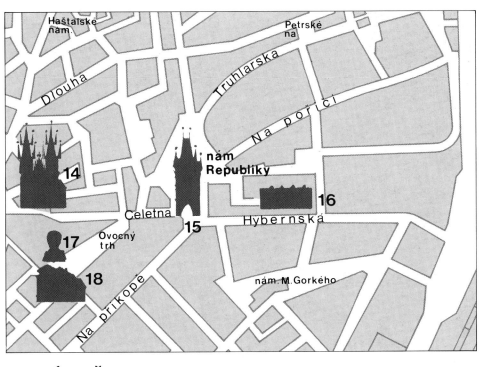

NOVÉ MĚSTO - THE NEW TOWN

The New Town was founded by Charles IV in 1348 to create extra market space and to house the increasing number of craftsmen drawn to Prague by the city's blossoming economy. The scale of its conception was quite remarkable with strict regulations laid down governing the standard of construction work and completion clauses built into the contracts, stating that work had to commence within a month and be completed within a year and a half. Similar impetus was given to the construction of the town's fortifications which after only two years ran for almost three kilometres, containing the plots laid out between the Old Town and the Castle at Vyšehrad. Today only the section running from here up to the Church of Our Lady and Charlemagne at Karlov remain, but they are imposing enough to remind us of the power and influence that the mediaeval city enjoyed.

The commercial heart of the New Town was centred around two main squares whose dimensions, even to the modern eye, are quite staggering. **Wenceslas Square** (Václavské náměstí) is 680 metres long and 60 metres wide. Although it has the appearance today of a large boulevard, and architecturally nothing has survived from its Gothic heyday, its bustling jam of shoppers denoting it as the consumer centre of contemporary Prague can't be very much different from the crowds that would have gathered here when it functioned as Charles's great Horse Market. Apart from the few remaining Art Nouveau facades, such as that of the beautiful Hotel Europa and the early twentieth-century equestrian statue of St. Wenceslas, there is little of any great artistic interest remaining in the Square. Even the dramatic buildings of the Neo-Classical National Museum (1885-90) seem slovenly and overbearing, which, given the immensity of the square they close, is really saying something. The architect of the

Following page
Wenceslas Square.

Hotel Europa: light fittings in the coffee bar.

project, Josef Schulz, also assisted on the construction of the slightly earlier National Theatre at the end of Narodni, next to the Bridge of Legions. But this is a far more successful attempt at creating a Neo-Renaissance building and a fitting symbol of the Czech nation's determination to provide itself with its own cultural milieu. Prior to this, Prague's theatres, including the Tyl in the Old Town, were German run and catered exclusively for a German-speaking audience. In 1845 a request for funding to build a new Czech Theatre was rejected by the now German dominated Estates. In response a nationwide appeal was launched to raise the necessary finance: the site was purchased and in 1881 the National Theatre opened with its first performance of Smetana's *Libuše*. Only two months later the newly completed Theatre was burned down, but it is a testament to the Czech people's resolve to provide their nation with this facility that it was rebuilt and reopened within two years.

Overall, very little remains from the period of the town's foundation. This is the result partly of the fact that the New Town, which housed the largest proportion of the city's poor, was the seedbed and stronghold of the Hussite radicals and therefore suffered to a greater extent from the reprisals of the anti-reform movement. There are, however, two churches founded at the same time as the town which have survived, albeit with certain modifications, down to the present. At the northern end of the square a small arcade cuts through into Jungmann Square where we find, secreted behinded an uninspiring cloister wall, the remarkable peace provided by the **Church of St.**

Left
Hotel Europa. After Paris and Vienna, Prague was the main centre for Art Nouveau and Secession.

115

Mary of the Snows. The name alone betokens the serenity of the building founded in 1347 as a monastic church for the Royal Coronation. The interior proportions of the church feel quite odd, the nave being so high in relation to its length that one could almost imagine oneself in the base of a huge tower. This is because the church was originally intended to be much larger, surpassing even St. Vitus Cathedral in size. However due to lack of funds and the interruption caused by the Hussite Wars, the building was never completed to plan, so that what we are left with now is a church made solely from the presbytery of the structure which was to have stretched the hundred metres to Jungmann Square itself. Situated right on the outskirts of Charles's New Town is the extraordinary **Church of the Assumption and Charles the Great** (Kostel Nanebevzetí Panny Marie a Karla Velikého). Construction started in 1358 on an octagonal plan based on that of Charlemagne's Palatine Chapel in Aachen and the church was consecrated in 1377. Although one can still imagine the essence of the Gothic building, especially in Wolmut's late sixteenth-century restoration of the ribbed stellar vaulting, the dome which marks it out from afar is the result of Baroque modifications.

The administrative centre of the New Town was the **New Town Hall** which still stands on Charles Square — the former Cattle Market. This was the scene for the act that sparked the turbulent period of the Hussite Wars. On 22nd July 1419, Jan Želivský, a Hussite radical, stormed the Town Hall at the head of an angry mob, demanding the release of fellow Hussites imprisoned in the buildings. When the councillors refused to comply with their demands, two of them were hurled from the window in what became known as the First Defenestration of Prague.

Charles Square, 530 metres in length by 150 metres in width, is the largest square in Prague. Today, however, its dimensions are deceptive, the area having been planted as parkland in the middle of the nineteenth century, at around the same time that the entire New Town underwent a wholesale redevelopment. It is still a good place to head to just for a wander and to sit and listen to the romantic rumble of trams as they course round the square, heading for all four corners of the city.

The Baroque **Church of St. Ignatius**, which dominates the square at the point where it is intersected by Ječná and Resslova, formed the centre of the Jesuit mission in the New Town along with the immense adjacent Jesuit College, surpassed in scale only by the Clementinum. A short distance away in Resslova stand two churches worthy of attention. The first, the Baroque **Church of Saints Cyril and Methodius**, is remembered as the last hiding place of the Czech resistance fighters responsible for the assassination of Reinhard Heydrich at Lidice in 1942. Having succesfully completed their mission they were cornered by the Nazis in the crypt of the church where they held out for some time before being overcome and shot. As a reprisal, the Nazis razed the outlying village of Lidice to the ground, executing all the men over the age of sixteen and deporting the women and children to concentration camps. A memorial tablet bearing the names of those who died in the crypt recalls the courage

The National Museum.

Following page
The National Theatre.

The National Theatre:
Proscenium arch and boxes.

Left
The stairwell of the National
Museum.

and heroism of their last days. Across the road stands the Gothic
Church of St. Wenceslas in Zderaz. Originally a Romanesque church,
elements of which are preserved in the west wall, it served the small
community of Zderaz which was subsequently incorporated into the
layout of the New Town. On a site slightly to the west of the church,
in Dittrichova, there originally stood a small castle, built for the use of
Wenceslas IV in about 1399. The bath building in the southernmost
portion of the castle existed through to the end of the nineteenth
century and was the scene in 1848 of a meeting called by the Czech
Repeal which led ultimately to the revolution of the same year.
Returning to Charles Square, head for Vyšehradská which makes an
exit in the south west. On the corner on the left as we leave the
square stands the originally Renaissance building known from the
seventeenth century as the **Faustus House**. The legend of a man who
sold his soul to the Devil for the temporal gratification of his body
originated in Germany in the late sixteenth century, but swiftly gained
popularity all through northern Europe.
The special quality of Prague, with her long history of multiracial co-
existence complemented by a corresponding architectural eclecticism, is
not easily forgotten. Czechs, Germans, Austrians, Italians and
Frenchmen have all left their mark in the cultural palimpsest of the
city. Prague is indeed a "threshold," not only to Central and Eastern
Europe but to new and vital experience.

CHRONOLOGY

c850 - 895   The Czech tribes are conquered by Duke Bořivoj, the first historically attested member of the Premyslid dynasty, who initiates the construction of Hradčany Castle.

874   Methodius, the Apostle of the Slavs, baptises Bořivoj. After his death his Christian wife, Ludmilla, is murdered thereby becoming Bohemia's first martyr and patron saint.

900 - 1000   Jewish, German, French and Italian merchants settle in Prague.

921   Ludmilla's grandson, Wenceslas, becomes Duke of Bohemia and builds the Rotunda of St. Vitus.

935   Wenceslas murdered by his brother Boleslav the Cruel.

973   Prague is elevated to the status of bishopric and Adalbert is invested as the first incumbent to the episcopal see.

993   Adalbert founds the Benedictine Abbey at Břevnov.

995   Premyslid domination is consolidated with the assassination of the Slavniks, the second most powerful family in Bohemia.

1085   Duke Vratislav II is crowned as the first King of Bohemia, a title granted to him by Emperor Henry V in gratitude for his assistance with the struggle for the investiture of Pope Gregory VII.

1140   Vladislav II founds the premonstratensian monastery at Strahov.

1158   Duke Vladislav II is awarded the hereditary title of King by Emperor Frederick Barbarossa in appreciation of his assistance against rebellious Northern Italian towns.

1170   Construction work starts on the Judith Bridge, the first stone bridge across the Vltava.

1178   Duke Soběslav II grants German merchants certain privileges as encouragement for them to stay in Prague. These include the right to be dealt with by German Law, tax incentives and exemption from military service.

1198   The Emperor raises Přemysl Ottakar I to the status of King.

1231   Under Wenceslas I the Old Town receives its municipal charter and is fortified with walls.

1232 - 1234   Eberhard, later to be Master of the Royal Mint, founds the Gall Town within the precinct of the Old Town walls.

1257   The area now known as Malá Strana is established by Přemysl Ottakar II as a German settlement governed by the Magdeburg legal code.

1306   The Premyslid dynasty dies out with the murder of Wenceslas III.

1310   After four turbulent years, during which the Habsburgs attempted unsuccesfully to take the throne of Bohemia for the first time, John of Luxemburg, husband to the Premyslid princess Elizabeth, fights his way into the city and becomes King.

c1320   Berka of Duba, the Burgrave of Prague Castle, founds a third town along the old road from Pohořelec to the castle and names it Hradčany.

1338   John of Luxemburg grants the inhabitants of the Old Town the right to build their own Town Hall in return for their financing of his foreign campaigns.

1344   Charles IV rules Bohemia as regent. Thanks to his benign relationship with the Holy See, he manages to raise Prague to an archbishopric and founds the Cathedral of St. Vitus.

1346   Charles IV becomes King of Bohemia.

1348   Charles founds his eponymous university together with the New Town which makes Prague the largest city in Central Europe.

1355   Charles becomes Holy Roman Emperor and Prague is raised to the capital city of the Holy Roman Empire.

1357   Charles builds a new stone bridge to replace the Judith bridge that had been swept away by a flood in 1342.

1360   Charles extends Malá Strana in a southerly direction and encloses it within a new wall.

1378 - 1419   During the weak reign of Wenceslas IV social unrest increases with a decline in the moral standards of the clergy.

1409   Prompted by Jan Hus, Wenceslas alters the voting structure within the university with the Decree of Kutná Hora, thereby giving the native Bohemians a distinct advantage over the Germans, many of whom leave the country in disgust.

1415   Jan Hus is summoned to the Council of Constance to defend his "heretical" views on the teaching of the Church. Refusing to retract his beliefs, he is burned at the stake despite having been guaranteed safe passage, thereby sparking off a vociferous, countrywide reaction to the established Church.

1419   A crowd led by Jan Želivský storms the New Town Hall demanding the release of imprisoned Hussite radicals. The councillors refuse and are hurled to their deaths from the windows in what became known as the First Defenestration of Prague.

1420   Pope Martin V issues a Papal Bull proclaiming a crusade against heretics in Bohemia, thereby instigating the period of the Hussite Wars. Between 1421 and 1431 a total of five crusades are launched against the Hussites by the combined forces of the Empire, all of which ended in humiliating defeat for the Holy Armies.

1436 - 71   George of Poděbrady emerges from the turmoil of the Hussite conflict and is elected King. In his desire to uphold the Compacts of Basle, which held the divergent Utraquists in a fragile peace with Rome, he was forced to play a skilful game of cut and thrust diplomacy, through which he secured the Bohemian succession for the friendly, Jagiellan dynasty in Poland.

1490   The domains of the Bohemian crown are united with those of Poland and Hungary as King Vladislav Jagiello transfers the capital from Prague to Buda.

1526   Ferdinand Habsburg is elected King of Bohemia, thereby establishing the dominion of the mighty Austrian family which was to last right up to 1918.

1541   Renaissance rebuilding of Prague takes place after a devastating fire in Hradčany and Malá Strana.

1549 onwards   The impetus of the Counter-Reformation, introduced into Bohemia by the Habsburgs, is tempered by the settling in Prague of a community of German Lutherans.

1556   Ferdinand I becomes Emperor and invites the Jesuits to Prague as missionaries for the Catholic conversion of the populace.

1575   The Bohemian non Catholic religious factions — predominantly the Neo-Utraquists, the Czech Brethren and the Lutherans — agree on the Czech Confession which was to replace the outmoded Compacts of Basle.

1583-1612   Czech culture profits from the temporary transfer of the Imperial Court from Vienna to Prague, which under Rudolf II becomes a centre for artistic and intellectual endeavour unparalleled since the days of Charles IV.

1609   In the face of overwhelming opposition from the Estates and his brother Matthias Corvinus in Hungary, Rudolf II finally capitulates and signs the Letter of Majesty, granting religious freedom to the Bohemians.

1611   On the abdication of Rudolf II, his brother Matthias becomes King.

1618   Catholic officials deliberately violate the terms of Rudolf's Letter of Majesty. In retribution they are thrown from the windows of the Bohemian Chancellery by members of the radical Protestant nobility in what became known as the Second Defenestration of Prague. This action results ultimately in the Thirty Years War.

1619   The Bohemian Estates reject the succession of Matthias's nephew Ferdinand II and choose instead Frederick V, Elector of the Palatinate, as King.

1620   Ferdinand II returns to Prague to claim his throne and utterly defeats the forces of the Bohemian Estates at the Battle of the White Mountain. Frederick V, known as the "Winter King" after his pitifully short reign, flees the city.

1621   Twenty-seven leaders of the Protestant anti-Habsburg uprising are executed on the Old Town Square.

1627   The Catholic faith becomes the only permissible religion. Those members of the nobility who refuse to adopt the Catholic faith are forced to emigrate leaving all their property behind, thereby reducing the population of Bohemia by one quarter.

1631   During the course of the Thirty Years War the Swedish army has advanced to the gates of Prague but is driven back by General Albrecht Wallenstein.

1648   The Peace of Westphalia seals the end of the Thirty Years War. Prague's economic and cultural importance diminishes rapidly.

1741-42   Occupation of Prague by Franco-Bavarian forces.

1781   Edict of Tolerance is passed by Joseph II. Programme of progressive reformation commences with the abolition of the monasteries.

1784   The Old Town, New Town, Hradčany and Malá Strana are united as a single administrative whole.

1848 An unsuccessful Czech nationalist uprising in the streets of Prague follows the authorities' refusal to grant equal rights for Czechs and Germans.

1861   The February Constitution cedes certain powers to the democratically elected Empire Council.

1882   Prague University is divided according to nationality.

1918   The Czechoslovak Republic is established albeit with its borders unconfirmed. The subsequent incorporation of Slovakia and the Sudetenland was to have far reaching consequences for the Czechoslovak State.

1938   In an atmosphere of appeasement the Munich Agreement is signed, thereby ceding the Sudetenland to Hitler's Germany.

1939   Hitler incorporates the rest of Czechoslovakia into the Nazi Protectorate of Bohemia and Moravia.

1945   The Czech government announces the Košice Programme for a socialist state, which, although it contained ideas similar to those expounded by President Beneš, was infused with communist content.

1948   The Communist Party assumes power in a bloodless coup. Czechoslovakia becomes a People's Republic.

1960   The Czechoslovak Socialist Republic is established.

1968   The period of liberalisation under Svoboda and Dubček, known as the Prague Spring, is brought to a violent end by the intervention of Warsaw Pact troops.

1989   On November 17th the people of Prague take to the streets and force the Central Council of the Communist Party to resign.

RESTAURANT LIST

If there is one single piece of advice that can be given to ensure a fulfilling stay, it is to *always* book restaurants at least two days ahead, especially for the evening meal. Of course there will be times in certain places when you can wander in off the street and get served, wondering what the fuss is about. Equally, if you don't book, there will be times when you simply wander the streets! Some places will not offer you a menu, stating that there are only three set courses available. If you feel reasonably confident with your ability to interpret a Czech menu then insist that you have one, unless you want your choice limited and, in some cases, your bill subject to the whim of the waiter. Although for obvious reasons Czech food is lacking in variety and fresh vegetables are almost unobtainable, with its emphasis on flour based recipes you will certainly not go hungry. If you like dumplings and lashings of gravy then you can't go far wrong with the specialities of chicken and duck served with red and white cabbage, or with the tempting palačinky — pancakes flambeed in alcohol and stuffed with fruit and ice cream.

Vikárka - Vikářská 6, Prague 1, Castle. Tel. 536497
Na Baště - Prague Castle, Prague 1. Tel. 537411.
Činská - Vodičkova 19, Prague 1, New Town. Tel. 262697.
Berjozka - Rytířská 7, Prague 1. Old Town. Tel. 228460.
Viola Trattoria - Národní tr. 7. New Town Tel. 266732.
Valdštejnská Hospoda - Valdštejnské Náměstí, 7, Prague 1. Malá Strana.
    Tel. 536195.
Nebozízek - Petřínské sady 411. Malá Strana. Tel 537905.
Europa - Hotel Europa - Václavské náměstí 9, Prague 1. Tel. 2365274. New
    Town
U zlatého jelena - Celetná 11, Prague 1 . Old Town Tel. 268595.
U zlaté hrušky - Nový svět 3 , Prague 1. Hradčany. Tel. 531133.
U mecenáše - Malostranské náměstí 10, Prague 1. Malá Strana Tel. 533881.
U Kolovrata - Valdštejnské náměstí 18, Prague 1. Malá Strana Tel. 536990.
U tří pštrosů - Dražického náměstí 12, Prague 1. Malá Strana Tel. 536007.
Parnas - Smetanovo nábřeží 2, Prague 1. New Town tel. 265017.
Opera Grill - Karolíny Světlé 35, Prague 1 . Old Town Tel. 265508.

KOSHER
Košer restaurace - Maislova 18, Prague 1. Jos. Tel. 2310909.

Vegetarian
Vegetárka - Celetná 3 , Prague 1. Old Town Tel. 2324605.

BEER HALLS (THOSE MARKED WITH ASTERISK ALSO SERVE FOOD)

Prague beer halls are on the whole noisy, smelly places, but then they do serve some of the best beer in the world such as Branik, Pilsen and Budvar. There are no crushing queues for the bar as the beers are almost thrown at you where you sit, with prompt service that borders on the clairvoyant ensuring that by the time you finish the first pint, the second will already be making its way across the room. It is unwise to slip into a pivnice for a late drink, however, as last orders are called around 9.30 and those seats that have been taken prior to this are usually occupied by people intending to stay for the duration.

U Šnellů * - Tomašská 2, Prague 1. Malá Strana Tel. 532004.
U Fleků * - Křemencova 9, Prague 1. New Town Tel. 293246.
U Kalicha * - Na bojišti, Prague 2. New Town Tel. 296017.
U Vejvodů * - Jilská 4, Prague 1. Old Town
U zlatého tygra - Husova 17, Prague 1. Old Town

WINE BARS

Although the term "vinárna" means wine bar in Czech, most of them now function purely as restaurants. U zelené žáby falls half way, as it does not serve full meals. However it is very popular, not least because of the succulent roast beef served on slices of golden fried bread, and should always be booked.

U zelené žáby - U radnice 8, Prague 1. Old Town Tel. 262815.
Lobkovická vinárna - Vlašská 17, Prague 1. Malá Strana Tel. 530185.
Klášterní Vinárna - Národní 8, Prague 1. New Town. Tel. 294863.

COFFEE BARS

Much of the coffee consumed in Prague is Turkish and very grainy, so if you like your caffeine Italian style you'll have to search quite hard. Listed below are some of the best and most well known places to sit and let the world revolve without you for a while.

Cafe Colombia - Mostecká 1, Malá Strana.
Europa - Václavske náměstí 29, New Town.
A Scena Espresso - Novotného Lávka, Old Town. (Open till 2.00am)
Kavárna Týn - Staroměstské náměstí, Old Town.
Malostranská Kavárna - Malostranské náměstí, Malá Strana.
Obecní Dům - Náměstí Republiky 2, Old Town.
Slavia - Národní třída 1, Old Town.

NIGHTCLUBS

As with the restaurants, if you wish to be sure of getting in (especially on a Friday night which is Prague's big night out), it is advisable to book.

Barberina - Melantrichova 10, Old Town. Tel 261084 (Open till 3.00am.
 Excellent for late food)
U bílého Koníčka - Staroměstské náměstí 20, Old Town. (Open till 3.00am.
 Some of the best dancing to be had in Prague)
Hanavský Pavilon - Letenské sady 173, Praha 7. Tel 325792
Rock Cafe - Národní Třída 20, Praha 1. Tel. 206656 (Open till 3.00am. Live
 music.)

JAZZ CLUBS
Press Jazz Club - Pařížská 9, Praha 1. Tel 2322618.
Reduta Jazz Club - Národní Třída 20, Praha 1. Tel 203825.

*Well Tower and Castle
walls.*